THE MOMMY SHORTS GUIDE TO

REMARKABLY AVERAGE PARENTING

THE MOMMY SHORTS GUIDE TO
REMARKABLY AVERAGE PARENTING

Ilana Wiles

Editor: Rebecca Kaplan
Designer: Amy Sly
Production Manager: True Sims

Library of Congress Control Number: 2016930108

ISBN: 978-1-4197-2219-6

Printed and bound in the United States

10 9 8 7 6 5 4 3 2 1

Abrams Image books are available at special discounts when purchased in quantity for premiums and promotions as well as fundraising or educational use. Special editions can also be created to specification. For details, contact specialsales@abramsbooks.com or the address below.

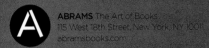

ABRAMS The Art of Books
115 West 18th Street, New York, NY 10011
abramsbooks.com

To Mazzy, Harlow, and Mike —
I think I've always been a writer, but you guys
gave me something I loved enough to write about

CONTENTS

INTRODUCTION

OVER THE PAST SIX YEARS, I have written about parenting on my blog, *Mommy Shorts*. I write about my struggles, my successes, my mistakes, my moments of joy, and now, six years in, with two adorable daughters STILL ALIVE, I can say with semiconfidence that I know a little bit about what I am doing.

I am not a good mother. I'm not a bad mother, either. I'm average. I love my kids more than life itself, but I am not always up for playing with them. Especially when they were toddlers. You're putting squares into square holes in a shape sorter. And they can't even do it! It's excruciating.

This book is for parents (and parents-to-be) who think parenting is tough but still believe they can have a pretty good time. Or NEED to believe, for their own survival.

I am not going to try to get you to be a better parent. I am here to tell you that you can get through parenting in a half-assed average way, frame it as bringing up independent kids who can think for themselves, and then tell everyone you are a FANTASTIC parent.

Actually, don't tell anyone that. Nobody wants to be friends with a parent who brags about their parenting skills. That's Mom Friend 101.

Owning "average" makes parenting fun. You don't have to do anything differently. You just have to see your pain as entertainment. You know how they say comedians often have inner struggles and use humor as a coping mechanism? Parenthood is your opportunity to become a comedian!

It's like you're part of a big club that nobody wants to belong to but all you have to do is

You have to love your kids, embrace the madness, find the humor, create your own entertainment, and laugh together as an entire community of people who have NO IDEA WHAT THEY ARE DOING.

whip out a bottle of wine and a well-timed joke about potty training and suddenly you have fifty new friends!

Actually, never use the term "whip out" among parents and children. You might get arrested.

What was I saying again? Oh, yes.

You have to love your kids, embrace the madness, find the humor, create your own entertainment, and laugh together as an entire community of people who have NO IDEA WHAT THEY ARE DOING. You can do this even in your worst parenting moments.

In fact, that's when things are at their most hilarious.

I might be an average parent, but I have also been blessed with a smart, nonjudgmental audience of fellow moms and dads who have reminded me time and time again that we are all going through the same things together. They have given me advice and support every step of the way. This book is not just my experiences (although that's most of it); it also takes advantage of all the knowledge and empathy I have gleaned from my readers over the years.

So yeah, you will learn a lot from this book. But maybe not all of it from me.

12 REJECTED TITLES
★ FOR MY ★
MOMOIR

1 The Good, the Bad, and the Time I Stepped on a LEGO

2 My Life and All the Noses I've Blown

3 "I Left Your Blankie at Home" and Other Devastating Tales of Motherhood

4 Don't Jump on the Baby: Life Lessons For My Eldest Daughter

5 Unidentified Stains: One Mom's Mission to Leave Her House Without Spit-Up on Her Shirt

6 I LOVE PARENTHOOD! (The TV Show; Real Life Parenthood Is Just Okay)

7 The X-haustion Files

8 Tangled Car Seat Straps: The Story of a Mom, a Dad, and the Family Road Trip that Almost Killed Them

9 Sorry Sweetie, Calliou's Dead

10 MOMONOMICS: How Laundry Multiplies While You Sleep

11 The Good Boob: A Tribute to the Side that Kept the Baby Alive

12 Wake Me When They Graduate

1

BECOMING A MOM

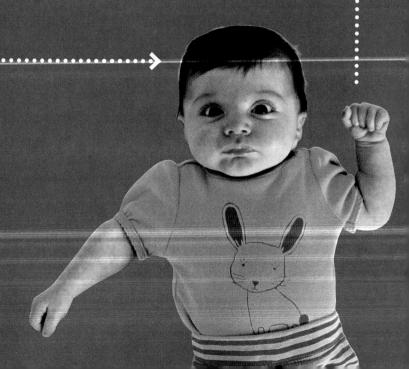

CHAPTER 1

So, You're Pregnant

I remember the day I found out I was pregnant. I peed on a stick, saw the plus sign, called my husband, and we celebrated just like you see on TV!

No, that's not true. There were doctor appointments and acupuncture and medication and a miscarriage and then POOF—I was with child! Neither easy nor anything I would start an infertility support group about. It was somewhere in the middle, as I've come to realize most parents fall.

But no matter whether you've been trying to conceive for years or you touched a penis once and got pregnant by magic, once you're expecting, everyone is in the same boat. Knocked up and at the doctor more than you ever thought possible.

And it's not just the number of times you're at the doctor, it's also the number of hours you're left freezing in a paper smock, waiting for your OB to enter the room. One time, my doctor forgot I was there and I was left sitting naked next to my own cup of urine for over an hour. If you told me I had an hour to do whatever I wanted, I think it's safe to say that staring at my own cup of urine would fall pretty low on that list. At least I had my iPhone to keep me and my urine company.

SERIOUS QUESTION: How were people pregnant in the days before they could read their phones **while waiting for the OB?** I mean, sure, it must have sucked to give birth before epidurals, but I'd be even more frightened to be an expectant mom alone with my own thoughts in the OB waiting room. That's when I'd start imagining every worst-case scenario possible, fall into a pregnancy disaster spiral, and start blaming myself for my unborn baby's future anxiety issues that surely transfer straight from the brain to the womb.

Want to hear something I never told anybody?

I thought my fetus had a big nose.

Can you think of a worse way to enter motherhood than doubting the attractiveness of your daughter before she is even born? And what's worse is that my own mother saw my ultrasound and confirmed all my suspicions by saying, "Looks like she'll need a nose job when she turns thirteen!" Then I yelled at my mom for being the most insensitive, superficial person alive, when really I had already researched how old my unborn baby would have to be before she could fix her obscenely large nose.

Here's a look at my Google search history from my first trimester:

★ *Can you tell the size of a baby's nose from an ultrasound?*

★ *Is it normal for a baby's nose to look especially large on an ultrasound?*

★ *Is it possible for a fetus to have a large nose but the actual baby's nose looks perfectly normal?*

★ *Can a baby get a nose job?*

Yep, pregnant women in their first trimester are CRAZY. I don't know if it's all the hormones or we've really been crazy all along and suddenly we're in a situation where it's expected and socially acceptable. Pregnancy is like a Get Out of Jail Free card to yell at your husband, make psycho demands at a restaurant, cut the bathroom line, run out of a boring meeting (just hold your hand over your mouth like you are seconds away from vomiting on the conference table)—basically all the things you've always wanted to do but feared rejection from society at large.

Once, I made my husband, Mike, have appetizers at one restaurant (they had gazpacho, my pregnancy craving) and then switch to another restaurant for the main course. This would have caused us to divorce on a normal night, but since I was carrying his child, he was happy to accommodate me.

Well, maybe "happy" is a little strong. Let's just say he didn't complain.

At least to me.

Your Odd Relationship With Food

Pregnant women fall into one of two camps—they want to eat everything or they want to eat nothing. I fell into the latter category, which was weird because I spent my entire life trying not to binge-eat everything within arm's reach, and then there I was, force-feeding myself saltines so I wouldn't pass out.

Almost everything made me nauseous during my first pregnancy. Except carbs, which I had been denying myself since the late nineties in the hope of one day achieving the perfect bikini body. (Thanks, Atkins, it never happened.) I was also a vegetarian who stopped eating meat as part of an environmental ethics class I took in college. I stuck with it because I found fault with the farming of animals, particularly the cruel treatment of cows in America's meat industry. I'm just kidding—I stuck with it because I was hoping that might also help me achieve the perfect bikini body. (That didn't work, either.)

> I can totally still do my job! After I take a nap on top of this file cabinet over—zzzzzzzzzzzz.

At the end of my first trimester, Mike and I took a trip to Paris. (I believe they call this a "babymoon," but I refuse to use that term, just like I refuse to use the Italian terminology at Starbucks.) In Paris, my food options were very limited and I began to worry my baby wasn't getting enough nutrients. I decided the best thing was to reintroduce chicken, but the thought made my stomach turn. Mike suggested taking the edge off with some bread—effectively breaking two of my food restrictions at once. We went to a tiny roadside *boulangerie* and I checked out the offerings. After a solid twenty minutes of deliberation, I opted for sliced chicken and tomato on a baguette, sat down on a bench, and took a bite. It was PERFECT. I remember describing to Mike exactly why the combination was so successful when he cut me off—"It's called a SANDWICH. People have been eating them since the beginning of time."

From that point forward, I was all about sandwiches, pizza, and pasta, and I never looked back. So, besides my kids, I have pregnancy to thank for making me eat like a normal human being again.

Working While Pregnant

I'm not sure, if in the twenty-first century, pregnant career women are supposed to admit to being less than 100 percent on the job, so this is a little tricky to talk about. I'm also pretty sure not every woman feels the same while pregnant, so I will just talk from my own experience.

At the office, where I had steadily risen up the ladder over the course of thirteen years to a pretty successful position for a woman of my age, I felt like I had to prove my worth and dedication like I was at square one. I had absolutely no intention of ending my career for motherhood, but what's a pregnant working girl to do when she can barely hold her head up past two p.m.?

"I can totally still do my job! After I take a nap on top of this file cabinet over—*zzzzzzzzzzzz*."

Otherwise, being pregnant at the office is very exciting. People who previously never asked you a thing about your sex life suddenly have the inside scoop. Everyone from the accounting department to human resources knows you had sex at least once and roughly at what time. And so many questions and comments! Almost all of them inappropriate. Or they have totally normal questions and comments that make you feel uncomfortable anyway.

Here's a tip: If you see a pregnant person, whether she is a coworker or your sister, just keep your mouth shut. There is literally not one thing you can say to a woman feeling large and conspicuous that will go over well.

WHAT PEOPLE SAY TO A PREGNANT WOMAN	WHAT A PREGNANT WOMAN HEARS
"Wow."	"You look HUGE."
"You look adorable."	"You look adorably HUGE."
"You look awesome."	"You look awesomely HUGE."
"You look so . . . FERTILE."	"I would like to have sex with you even though you are HUGE."
"You're really starting to pop!"	"It's only a matter of time before you get HUGE."
"I didn't know you were pregnant."	"I just thought you were HUGE!"
"How many months are you?"	"This is my polite way of asking if you are supposed to look so HUGE."
"You are carrying well."	"It's amazing you can still walk, what with being so HUGE."
"You look like you are about to pop!"	"HOLY CRAP!!!! I HAVE NEVER SEEN ANYONE PREGNANT OR OTHERWISE SO FREAKIN' HUGE!!!!!"

Finding Out The Sex Of The Baby

Some people like surprises, some people hate surprises, and some people find out the gender of their baby because they have a genetic condition that predisposes the baby to something horrible but the chances of the baby having it go way down if the baby is a girl so they find out for peace of mind.

Yeah, I know, not the answer you want to hear when you bring this up as a fun topic of discussion with a pregnant woman you just met in line at the grocery store. This is why you should refer to the section on the previous page and never talk to pregnant people. Whether their baby bump looks adorable or not, many of them are dealing with some tough fucking shit.

We found out the sex of our baby for the genetic reason previously mentioned (which ended up not being an issue at all) and also because Mike really wanted a boy and needed to be prepared if his dreams weren't coming true.

I believe his actual words were "If we have a girl, I don't want my first reaction to her to be disappointment."

Yeah, I didn't write that one in the baby book.

NOTE TO MAZZY AND HARLOW (spoiler alert: my two girls): If you are reading this—do not worry. Your father is just super honest and pragmatic and he was right to find out first, because he got over the whole disappointment thing real quick. He loves you both more than life itself and has since Day One.

As for me, I convinced myself that I didn't care about the sex of the baby until the day of our twenty-week ultrasound when I was lying on the table watching the technician calculate all the measurements and thinking, *Forget the size of the head. Just tell me if it's a girl!* Every time I saw something resembling an appendage, I found myself chanting internally, "Please don't be a penis, please don't be a penis, please don't be a penis . . ."

It was not a penis.

YAY!!!!!!!!!!!!!!!!

I mean, um . . . Mike? Are you going to be OK?

Mike needed a moment of silence to mourn the loss of his son before getting excited about having a daughter. Thankfully, that moment was brief.

Then we had to go about the very important task of giving our baby girl a name.

Naming A Baby Is Easy, If You Don't Have A Husband

If you are anything like me, you've been plotting your baby's possible names since you were about thirteen. For the first few years, my list existed only in my head, but once I got my first computer, the list was transferred from my brain to an actual Word document, hidden within a folder within a folder within a folder, just in case a boyfriend ever started poking around my desktop. Wouldn't want him to realize I was CRAZY before we got a chance to make the babies I had already named, now would we?

Mike thinks we came up with Mazzy's name together, but if he were to look back through my computer archive from, say 1995, he would see that Mazzy was on the top of my list all along. I think it started with me glancing at a Mazzy Star CD back in college and thinking—hmmmm . . . that would make an awesome name!

Thank god for Mazzy, because otherwise Mike and I couldn't reach an agreement on names at all. My husband thinks every name sounds like a stripper or a cat. If not a stripper or a cat, then he has some weird association with it that makes the name unusable. Like teachers he hated or bullies who tripped him in the lunchroom or horrible ex-girlfriends. ("Horrible" is my word, not his.) Seriously, how many times can a man nix a name because it belongs to an ex-girlfriend before I start wondering if my husband used "has legs" as his only dating criteria?

My husband thinks every name sounds like a stripper or a cat.

Here's an example of a naming conversation (pre-gender reveal) between my husband and me:

ME: What do you think of Rowan?

MIKE: No.

ME: What's wrong with Rowan? Rowan is a cool kid!

MIKE: No, he's not. He's a British comedian who wears his pants too short.

ME: What? What are you talking about?

MIKE: You know, that guy. Rowan Atkinson.

ME: Mr. Bean???

MIKE: Yeah, I'm not naming my kid Mr. Bean.

ME: All right, what about Lennon for a girl?

MIKE: No. Then everybody's going to think we're huge Beatles fans, start asking fifties music trivia questions, and we're not going to know the answers to any of them.

ME: The Beatles started in the sixties.

MIKE: Exactly.

ME: What about Lennox?

MIKE: Lennox is a stripper.

ME: What about Archer for a boy?

MIKE: Archer is cool.

ME: And then we can call him Archie for short!

MIKE: You just ruined it for me.

ME: Sebastian?

MIKE: Sebastian is a cat.

ME: Jasper?

MIKE: Jasper is a ghost.

ME: That's Casper.

MIKE: Same thing.

ME: Allegra?

MIKE: Allegra is an allergy medication.

ME: You come up with something.

MIKE: Indiana.

ME: That's pretty!

MIKE: Indiana Jones Wiles.

ME: YOU SUCK.

1000 WEIRD BUT NOT TOO WEIRD BABY NAMES

I'm pretty proud of the names we ultimately picked for our girls. Mazzy and Harlow are weird enough so that very few people choose to use them, but not too weird where everyone thinks Mike and I are monsters for giving our children outlandish names.

That's the naming sweet spot, in my opinion.

I didn't always feel that way. Two days after Mazzy was born, a good friend of mine visited and greeted my newborn with "Hi, Spazzy Mazzy!"

"WHAT DID YOU JUST SAY???"

"Didn't you test her name for bad rhymes so you'd be prepared for what she'll be called on the playground one day?"

"Noooooooo. . . ."

I had not heard about the rhyme test. It wouldn't have even occurred to me, since Mazzy was my chosen name for the past fifteen years. I was . . . How do I put this lightly? DEVASTATED. In only the way a brand-new mom can be. **I HAD FAILED MY VERY FIRST PARENTING TASK!!!**

Those first few weeks, I remember lying awake at night trying to think of all the other totally normal names that rhyme with something bad— Smelly Kelly, Icky Ricky, Cooper the Pooper, Tucker the Fucker, etc.

There were a few more people who criticized our odd choice of name those first few months. I took it really hard, because self-doubt is a huge part of being a new mom. Eventually, I made peace with Mazzy and remembered all the reasons I'd loved the name for so many years. It suits our daughter perfectly.

So, my advice to you would be: If you want to name your child something odd, I support you. I like odd names. I think odd names make the world a more interesting place. But you should be prepared to hear some criticism when you are at your most vulnerable.

And if you forget to give your name the rhyme test?

Thank Esther the Molester for helping you sleep at night.

Love It Or Hate It

Eventually, you become a seasoned pregnant person. You know to carry a bag of crackers around with you at all times. You know which commercials make you cry and how many times you'll wake up in the middle of the night to pee. You've decorated and redecorated your nursery at least twice. Your belly button has turned inside out, revealing what seems to be a decades-old substance. You are in the homestretch.

Once you hit your third trimester, most pregnant women will take one of two positions: **1)** Pregnancy sucks and I want this baby out of me yesterday. **2)** Pregnancy is the most amazing experience ever and I am so proud to be a woman and see what my body is capable of. I didn't really fall into either camp. Saying it sucks seems overly dramatic and saying it's beautiful might be true, but it kinda makes me want to gag. Pregnancy is indeed amazing, but for totally different reasons than most women talk about.

10 REAL REASONS YOUR THIRD TRIMESTER IS AWESOME

1 If you've spent your whole life trying to hide your less than flat stomach (as I have), suddenly you are totally comfortable having it on full display.

2 When making restaurant/take-out/dinner decisions with a group of friends/coworkers/relatives, everybody always defers to you to make the final call.

3 You can use "I'm not feeling up to it" to get out of pretty much anything—household chores, visiting friends all the way across town, bedtime routine with your toddler, etc.

4 You can send your husband out on emergency errands like "It's eleven p.m. and I need Twizzlers!" or "I know we have five cartons of ice cream in the freezer but none of them are *Ben and Jerry's Americone Dream!!!*"

5 If an old person gets on the bus/train/subway, you don't have to be the one to give up your seat.

6 You can alternate between the same two outfits for three months and nobody bats an eye.

7 Random strangers smile at you on the street and it's not that creepy. You actually kind of like it. (As long as they don't try to touch you.)

8 Bathroom lines magically part for you, restaurant employees allow you to use their facilities even if you wandered in off the street and have no intention of eating there, and Broadway theater ushers will pick you out of obscenely long intermission bathroom lines and escort you to magical private bathrooms you never knew existed. (It's true! I was there!)

9 Nobody ever expects you to carry anything.

10 You may look and feel like a whale, but it's a whale with AMAZING HAIR.

It's Almost Over

With my first baby, I gave birth ten days early. This was a blessing because it was a total surprise and I never spent those last few weeks/days agonizing over when or where it was going to happen.

With my second, I gave birth on my due date and the waiting (although uneventful) was excruciating.

This is the time I recommend getting a haircut, getting a mani-pedi, seeing a few movies (which will be your last non-animated movies for the next five to ten years), having brunch with your girlfriends, etc.

Otherwise, your last few days will look like the chart below.

And if you make it to forty-one weeks with no new news, induce that shit. That baby is cooked and the bigger it gets, the more you risk breaking your vagina when it comes out.

BEING 40 WEEKS PREGNANT IS...

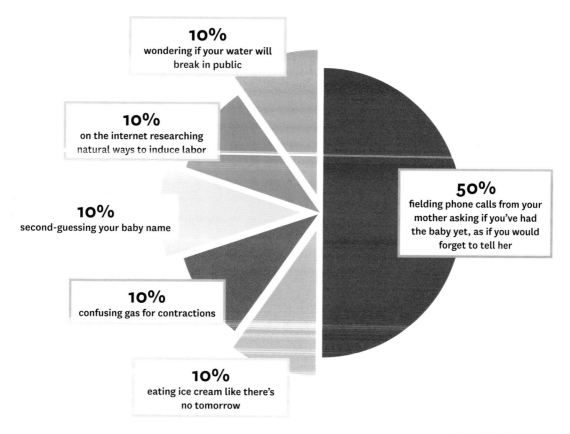

10%
wondering if your water will break in public

10%
on the internet researching natural ways to induce labor

10%
second-guessing your baby name

10%
confusing gas for contractions

10%
eating ice cream like there's no tomorrow

50%
fielding phone calls from your mother asking if you've had the baby yet, as if you would forget to tell her

CHAPTER 2 Contractions, Epidurals, And Placentas, Oh My

Congratulations, you have a baby! Well, not yet. There's still that small detail of actually giving birth. Will you go the natural route or get an epidural? Will your spouse rise to the occasion or will you scream obscenities at him like pregnant women do in the movies? Will you get to the hospital on time or will you wind up on the morning news as the mom who gave birth on the side of the highway with only the light of her husband's iPhone to make sure everything was A-OK?

Literally nothing in your life will be as dramatic as the day you push a small alien out of your insides and then attempt to feed it with your boob. Birth is amazing, yeah sure, whatever. But also PAINFUL and REALLY FUCKING WEIRD.

I know people say that the day your baby's born will be the most beautiful day of your life, but I disagree. Holding my baby for the first time was awesome, but the WHOLE FREAKIN' DAY? I don't think so.

You know what was a beautiful day? My wedding. Yes, more beautiful than the day I gave birth. And I think if you put your wedding day and the day your baby was born in head-to-head competition, you'll have no choice but to agree.

While I was pregnant, I remember wondering if the act of giving birth would flip all negative emotion off and turn me into this ethereal being overcome with love and the profound opportunity to be someone's mother.

But no, I was still myself when I delivered my baby. A cynic who sees things for what they are. Yes, I felt the need to love and protect this tiny being that was suddenly in my arms, but I also felt totally freaked out.

I mean—I just produced a person! Who entered the world through my vagina! And now I was required to make sure that tiny creature went to college!

I've read a lot of things about women feeling elated after birth and about women feeling depressed after birth, but I don't think either is the most common experience. I think most women feel a mix of all different emotions and then they compound these emotions by wondering if this is how they are supposed to feel. The answer is (in my totally unmedical opinion), there is no one way a brand-new mom is supposed to feel after she gives birth.

10 TOTALLY ACCEPTABLE FEELINGS TO HAVE AFTER BIRTH

1. Is my baby cute? I'm not sure if she's cute. Yes, she's cute. She kind of looks like a wrinkly old man, but a cute wrinkly old man.

2. I love my wrinkly old-man baby!

3. Can somebody clean this thing up so I don't get my insides all over my hair?

4. That was way harder than I thought it was going to be.

5. That was way easier than I thought it was going to be.

6. I don't think I'm ready for this.

7. I'm exhausted. Can someone put this baby in the nursery so I can catch some *zzzzzs*?

8. No way I am parting with this baby ever. In fact, I'm getting nervous with her over there getting cleaned up by the nurses. DON'T DROP HER!!!!!

9. Yay! She scored a 9 on her Apgar test! Wait—why didn't she get a 10? Oh shit. Am I going to be one of those overachiever moms who pressures her kid to get into Harvard and ultimately drives her away for good????

10. Oh phew. My baby's nose does not look nearly as big as it did on the ultrasound.

The Day Mazzy Was Born

I stood up and immediately felt my stomach tighten.

"Oh."

"What?" Mike asked. He was still in bed.

"I just felt a crampy thing. I think it was a Braxton Hicks."

"A Braxton what?"

"Do you pay attention in the class AT ALL?"

Mike chose to ignore me and asked instead, "What are you gonna do with your first day off?"

It was Monday morning, about two weeks before my due date, and it was the first weekday morning since I had taken off work.

"I'm going to the gym and then I'm meeting Lauren for lunch."

At the gym, I went for a run on the treadmill. I had been very active throughout my pregnancy, which is totally laughable considering how little time (and by little, I mean none) I make for the gym now.

At lunch, I sat across from my newly divorced friend as she regaled me with various online dating stories and the occasional question about my impending child.

"Do you feel like you're ready to have the baby?"

> I debated waking him but decided to let him sleep. After all, it would be his last chance for uninterrupted sleep EVER.

"No, not at all."

After lunch, I went to Trader Joe's. It was a ten-block walk to the store. Once there, I started feeling the Braxton Hicks again, so just for fun I took out my iPhone and loaded the iContractions app. I thought this would be a good test run for the real thing.

As I walked around the store picking up frozen raspberries and bell peppers, I recorded my "tightenings" on the phone. I left with five full bags and proceeded to lug them back to my apartment. Each time I felt something, I stopped, put the bags down, input the time into my app, and waited for the feeling to pass before I kept walking.

When I finally got home (which took a while, considering all the bags and the stopping), I looked at my phone.

Huh. Each "tightening" was exactly four minutes apart.

I called Mike.

"My phone says I'm in labor."

"I thought you said it was the Braxton Hicks."

"It might be. Do they occur in regular intervals?"

We both furiously googled "Braxton Hicks."

"Are you getting them right now?"

"No. It seems to have stopped."

"Well, then it's probably a false alarm."

I sat around my apartment playing with iContractions. The "tightenings" seemed to be getting more intense but less regular. And then more regular but less intense. But they definitely weren't going away.

I called Mike again. It was about four p.m.

"You should come home now."

About two hours later, Mike walks in the door with three huge bags from Duane Reade.

WHICH DAY IS THE BEST IN YOUR LIFE?	YOUR WEDDING DAY	THE DAY YOUR BABY WAS BORN
WHAT YOU'RE WEARING		
WHERE YOU'RE LOCATED		
WHO'S KEEPING YOU COMPANY		
WHAT YOU'RE EATING		
WHAT YOU'RE EATING FOR DESSERT		
WHAT YOU LOOK LIKE		
WHAT YOUR HUSBAND LOOKS LIKE		
VERDICT	IF IT WASN'T FOR TAKING HOME THAT BABY . . . ALTHOUGH, THE BREAD MAKER NEVER CRIES.	

"What the hell is that?"

"We needed toilet paper and paper towels."

"Your very pregnant wife tells you to COME HOME NOW and you go to the drugstore to buy paper products?"

"How are you feeling?"

"I have no idea."

Mike and I sat side by side on the couch, each with our laptops, googling the difference between "real labor" and "false labor."

Mike delivered his now expert opinion.

"I think you are in false labor."

I delivered mine: "I think it's the real thing."

"If you think it's real labor, then call the doctor."

"Is that some sort of challenge?"

Mike shrugged.

"Fine! I will call the doctor!"

I called the doctor. The nurse's station answered. I described what was happening. She told me that I didn't sound like I was in that much pain (apparently, I was talking too easily) and should wait to come in.

In an uncharacteristically gallant show of support, Mike didn't say "I told you so." I turned on the TV and Mike proceeded to fall asleep on the couch. (Of course he did. It's not like anything exciting was happening.) I debated waking him but decided to let him sleep. After all, it would be his last chance for uninterrupted sleep EVER.

I finished packing our hospital bag. I tried everything imaginable to make myself more comfortable. Leaning over the couch. Lying on the floor. Curling into the fetal position. I even pressed a tennis ball into my back (on recommendation from a friend), which was, ultimately, the only thing that helped defuse the pain.

Eventually, the pain got so intense, I didn't want to deal with it on my own. Plus, the repeat episode of *Law & Order* was over.

I woke Mike up. It was two a.m.

"It's time to go to the hospital."

My husband is at his absolute worst when he is awakened from a deep sleep. He looked at me like he was hearing I was pregnant for the very first time. Then the previous evening (and the past nine months) came slowly back to him.

"The teacher said to wait as long as possible before you go to the hospital, because if you are not far enough along, they will just send you home," he offered.

"Yes, I know. Why do you think I let you sleep for the past FIVE hours? LET'S GO."

We went downstairs. It was pouring out.

Mike: "I have to get a cup of coffee."

Me: "Seriously?"

Mike: "I'll just go to the bodega across the street. Wait here."

The night doorman looked at me with total and complete terror. I grabbed my tennis ball, bent over the lobby couch, and pressed.

Mike returned about fifteen minutes later.

"Sorry I took so long, I had to wait for them to brew a fresh pot."

"YOU WAITED FOR THEM TO BREW A FRESH POT??! ARE YOU OUT OF YOUR MIND? WHAT EXACTLY DO YOU THINK IS GOING ON HERE???"

The doorman gave me a sad smile. It was pity, I'm sure.

When we got to the hospital, the nurse told us they were filled to capacity and to sit in the waiting room.

I spent the next three hours leaning over a bench with my butt high in the air and my trusty tennis ball jammed in my side, wondering how many people had given birth in this waiting room.

When they finally admitted me, I was dilated to four centimeters.

Up until that point, I had been taking the whole thing in stride . . . but once I lay down in the hospital bed, **ALL HELL BROKE LOOSE.** I started shivering, the contractions went from zero to sixty, and I looked at Mike in total panic. I think this was the first time Mike realized we were actually having a baby.

He squeezed my hand, told me to breathe, and said it would be fine.

The nurses took me into another room, where I waited as patiently as possible for my epidural.

While I tell everyone who will listen to get an epidural, I have to say it was one of the hardest parts of my delivery, because you're trying desperately to stay still while your body wants to convulse like crazy. I was scared I would have a contraction midway through and lose the use of my legs forever, but I guess the doctors know what they are doing.

Once the epidural was administered and the drugs kicked in, it was about six a.m. All was well, but everything slowed down to a stop.

For the next twelve hours we sat in the room, watching television, entertaining family and friends (who had called all these people to tell them I was here???), and generally relaxing. It was like a BIRTHING BIZARRO WORLD.

At six p.m., the doctor administered Pitocin to get the contractions going again.

Two minutes later, I was surrounded by a team of hospital staff telling me to push. It felt incredibly strange to be part of the same intense scene you have seen played out in the movies and on

He looked at me like he was hearing I was pregnant for the very first time.

episodes of *Grey's Anatomy* a billion times. Like living your very own cliché.

After the first push, the doctor said, "Great job! You will have this baby in no time!"

I pushed again.

The pushing process turned out to be way easier than I expected (I know nobody says that), and I couldn't stop laughing at myself through most of it.

"Do you want a mirror to see what's happening?" asked the nurse.

"NOOOO!!!" Mike and I both shouted in unison.

Two more pushes and she was out. It was Tuesday at 6:22 p.m.

"Do you want to hold her?"

I was supposed to say "Yes," right?

"Yes."

The nurse handed me a tiny pink baby with a full head of jet-black hair. Her eyes were puffy but open. I would be lying if I said it was anything but weird to hold the being that had been growing inside my uterus for the past nine months.

I studied her. She was pretty cute as far as newborns go.

"Hi."

Mike kissed the baby's forehead and then mine.

"She's ours," he said.

"Yes, she is."

Mazzy had the misfortune of being born pre-Instagram when I didn't take nearly as many photos. This is actually my second daughter, Harlow.

"Should we tell everybody her name?"

"Okay."

I will never forget the pride in my husband's voice as he announced his daughter to the doctors and nurses.

"SAY HELLO TO MAZZY ROSE!"

And my heart swelled for my little family of three.

9 EXAMPLES OF CRAP HUSBANDS PULL WHILE THEIR WIVES ARE IN LABOR

Once upon a time, I thought my husband abandoning me with my doorman so that he could run across the street to get a cup of freshly brewed coffee was totally egregious behavior for a dad-to-be. Then I asked my blog readers for examples of crap their husbands pulled while they were in labor, and I realized I got off pretty good.

1 "We live forty minutes from the hospital. As we were getting ready to walk out the door, my husband asked if I could drive." —Colleen

2 "My husband was playing video games when I went into labor. His reply when I told him it was time to go to the hospital: 'Okay, hang on, let me finish this level.'" —Skibby

3 "My husband took so many pictures of himself in the scrubs and mask, the camera battery was dead when we actually had the baby! I have the pictures to prove it." —Stephanie

4 "My husband started throwing up while I was pushing. The nurse ran out of the room because she couldn't handle it." —Lois

5 "A few hours after I gave birth, I asked my husband for one of the snacks I had packed in my hospital bag and he replied, 'Oops. I ate them all.'" —Gina

6 "I was in labor all night and ready to go in the morning. My husband had slept in a chair all night and when the nurse woke him up, he walked over to me and said, 'My foot hurts.' Really? Get this man an epidural." —Michelle

7 "At one point during labor with our first, a nurse asked my husband what my blood type is. He replied, '34B.'" —Angela

8 "I sent my husband home from the hospital to get me something comfortable to wear and he comes back with a T-shirt that says 'Wanna Play Doctor?' Mortifying." —Mallory

9 "I had a C-section. As the doctor pulled the baby from my stomach, my husband screamed, 'HE IS WHITE!!!' Well, yes, we are white people. But all the doctors and nurses stopped to look at both of us. Like my husband was unsure of the race of our baby. Needless to say, he has not lived that one down." —Kimberly

The First Night In The Hospital With Your Newborn

That first night with my newborn baby girl at my bedside was the most eye-opening night of my life. Since we didn't have a private room in the hospital, spouses were not allowed to stay overnight, so Mike went home and got a good night's sleep. All while I struggled to breast-feed and had a crash course on changing diapers. And I don't just mean my baby's diaper. I MEAN MY OWN.

Why does no one tell you about the puppy pads they make you wear in the hospital? Honestly, I think I would have preferred a real adult diaper. At least that would have been preconstructed by a professional. Instead, I'm half asleep, squirting water up my vagina while stuffing a pair of gauze panties with loose cotton and wrapping the crotch in a pad I had seen my sister use for her dogs on the floor. It's the twenty-first century! We carry all our music and TV shows in our pocket! Don't we have a better solution for post-birth panties????

Also, people had prepared me for the pain of labor, but nobody had prepared me for the pain after labor. So here you go: BE PREPARED FOR THE PAIN AFTER LABOR.

I felt like I had been run over by a truck. And my nether regions felt like they were dragging on the floor.

Everybody talks about the post-birth poop as being some sort of come-to-Jesus moment, but I don't remember the first poop. I do remember my vagina feeling so lifeless that I had absolutely no idea whether I was done peeing. I'd just sit there on the toilet thinking, *Should I get up now? If I try to stand up, will I immediately have to sit back down? If I make it all the way back to my bed, will I have to run right back to the bathroom?*

Making this bathroom excursion more complicated was the fact that I had opted to have my baby in the room with me the whole time. I'm not sure why when it would have cost no extra money to have the nurses watch her, but at that point in my momdom, I felt the need to prove I could do it myself. Plus, this is what the books suggested for BONDING, so I didn't want to screw up my child on her very first day of life.

The nurses told me that, in order to keep the baby in my room, I must never leave her unattended, even taking her with me when I used the bathroom. My guess is that this is to prevent baby theft, which seems like a rule you don't want to mess with. But I was also hooked up to an IV, so I had to wheel that in, too. So, instead of remembering the first time I tried to breast-feed or the first time my mom met my baby, my most vivid post-birth memories are trying to maneuver a huge bassinet on wheels around a crowded hospital room in the middle of the night without getting it tangled in my IV so I could retrieve my bin of puppy pads and squirt bottles and make it to the bathroom without peeing on the floor.

And then just sitting there on the toilet, having a heart-to-heart with my vagina, wondering if I was really done.

It's Time To Go Home

After the baby-care classes in the hospital, visits from the lactation specialist (why does she have such cold hands?), and watching the "Don't Shake the Baby" video, which is required for all new parents, the doctors usually tell you it is time to leave.

In some cases, they send Mom home without the baby, which is what happened to me. One doctor noticed trauma on Mazzy's eyes and wanted a specialist who wouldn't be in until the next day to check her out. Suddenly, I was released and our baby was not, and there was no way we were leaving without her. Mike and I broke the rules and spent the night sleeping in the waiting room.

The next day, after stressing out all day waiting for the doctor and then the results, Mazzy checked out fine and my baby was ready to come home.

And that's when shit got real.

I remember sitting on my living room floor surrounded by enough layette items to clothe quadruplets, examining my nipples for defects to explain why the baby wouldn't latch on, and wondering, *HOW THE HELL DID I GET HERE???*

But, squeeeeeeee!!!! Look at that cute little button nose!

This is really Mazzy.

CHAPTER 3

Are You Sure This Newborn Is Mine?

Not everybody has the luxury of being locked in a small apartment with her newborn for three months, desperately trying to keep the baby alive, while her husband does regular things like go to Chipotle with his work buddies, so I'm pretty sure I'm supposed to count myself lucky. I had a three-month paid maternity leave, which is actually way less than most countries, but every time I hear people say things like "Moms in the United States should get one year off like the people in Denmark!" I'm like—Hell, no! Three months was ENOUGH.

I mean, I wouldn't have traded that time for being at work. I'm very glad I had it. Getting to know my newborn without the pressure of checking work emails is a good thing. But first-time moms should be prepared: The newborn phase is NO PICNIC.

For starters, they tell you to keep your baby indoors for the first six weeks to avoid germs. But make sure you give them sufficient sunlight to avoid jaundice. But not too much sunlight, because you don't want to give them early onset skin cancer. Standing in front of a window should be fine. As long as that window wasn't washed recently with a nonorganic cleaning spray. THAT STUFF IS DEADLY.

All this conflicting info can drive a new mom crazy.

That craziness manifests itself in a sudden obsession with hand sanitizer (by the door, in the diaper bag, hanging from a string around your neck) and a fear of anyone other than yourself dropping the baby. Actually, I was most afraid

I would drop the baby. I was also afraid the umbilical cord stub would fall off prematurely, causing my baby to bleed out the belly button. I was afraid I'd chop off my baby's entire finger with a nail clipper. That she would suffocate in the baby carrier. And that her neck would bend so far back, her head would fall right off.

In hindsight, the newborn phase wouldn't be that hard if new parents weren't so worried about messing up in such a way that it would ruin their newborn's life forever. I'm not just talking about physical harm. I'm talking about mental harm, too.

How does one mentally harm their child?

You do something totally selfish like take a shower while you think your baby is napping.

THE 10 PHASES OF TAKING A SHOWER WITH A NEWBORN IN THE HOUSE

MINUTE ONE: Your newborn dozes off in the bouncer and you decide this is the perfect time to take a shower. You go to the bathroom and undress.

MINUTE TWO: You get nervous your baby will somehow figure out how to detach the strap holding her in the bouncer, giving her free rein of your house. The fact that she can't move is not important. You run back out of the bathroom (fully naked, I should mention) and successfully transfer the baby to her crib.

MINUTE THREE: You get in the shower. You allow yourself to appreciate the warm, cleansing water.

MINUTE FOUR: The baby starts crying. Wait. Is that crying? You aren't sure. You stick your head out of the shower and listen intently. You might be imagining it. You shampoo as quickly as possible just in case. You wash your body at lightning speed. The baby's cries get louder. Yes, that is definitely crying now. What about conditioner? Do you have time for conditioner?? You must get out as soon as possible. Wait! Have you shampooed yet? YOU CAN'T REMEMBER!!!

MINUTE FIVE: The baby's cries escalate to unbearable levels. OH MY GOD, THE BABY MUST THINK SHE HAS BEEN TOTALLY ABANDONED AND THIS TEN-MINUTE SHOWER IS GOING TO RUIN HER FOR LIFE!!!

MINUTE SIX: You turn the water off. There is complete silence. Did the baby stop crying or was she never crying to begin with? No matter. Time to condition. You turn the water back on.

MINUTE SEVEN: Why is the baby being so quiet??? Something must be wrong. You stick your head out of the shower and shout in the baby's direction. "BABY!!!!!! ARE YOU OKAY?????" The baby doesn't answer you. OH MY GOD, SOMETHING HAS HAPPENED TO MY BABY!!!!

MINUTE EIGHT: The baby starts crying again. OH THANK GOD.

MINUTE NINE: You emerge from the shower, naked and wet. You run to the baby, nearly slipping on the bathroom floor. You scoop her up in your arms. "OH, SWEETIE! I'M SO SORRY!!!!!! I'LL NEVER SHOWER AGAIN!!!!!"

MINUTE TEN: Shit. Is that still conditioner in my hair?

I DON'T ALWAYS SPIT UP MY LUNCH BUT WHEN I DO, I MAKE SURE IT GETS IN YOUR HAIR.

I DON'T ALWAYS SIT UP AND SMILE BUT WHEN I DO, IT'S AT 4 A.M.

I DON'T ALWAYS DROP MY PACIFIER BUT WHEN I DO, IT ROLLS ALL THE WAY UNDER THE COUCH.

I DON'T ALWAYS CRY FOR MY MOMMY BUT WHEN I DO, IT'S RIGHT WHEN SHE GETS IN THE SHOWER.

Breast-Feeding

Let me start by saying if you don't want to breast-feed or can't breast-feed for whatever reason (and there are tons of reasons), your baby will be just fine. I was formula-fed from the very beginning, and look at me! I wrote a book!

Learning to breast-feed (and no, I don't know anyone who just did it instinctually) opens up a whole host of questions:

* **Am I doing it right?**
* **Am I making enough?**
* **Are my nipples defective?**
* **Is my baby latching correctly?**
* **How can I tell if she is drinking anything?**

* **How many times a day am I supposed to do this again?**
* **Seriously?**
* **OH MY GOD, breast-feeding is a full-time job.**

They say breast-feeding is one of the best things you can do for your child. Even formula commercials tell you that. I believe they are required to tell you that by law. I'm not kidding—I've worked on formula commercials. Breast milk makes your babies smarter, less likely to get sick, more likely to say "I love you" as teenagers, less likely to go to jail, more likely to start a tech company that overthrows Facebook and makes your entire family gajillionaires, blah blah blah.

It also hurts like a bitch.

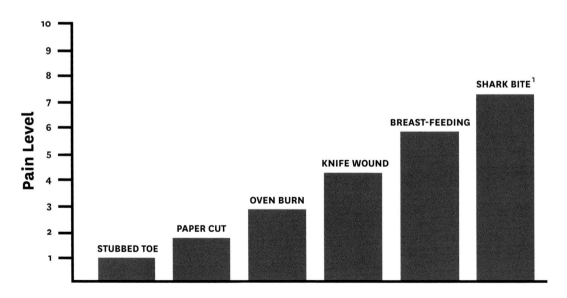

1 *It's entirely possible a shark bite is less painful than breast-feeding, but since I have never been personally bitten by a shark, I can operate only on assumption. If a shark has bitten you and you are qualified to make a more accurate comparison, please let me know.*

Even worse, there are people who say, "If it hurts, you are doing it wrong." That's crap and you shouldn't listen to them. I have not met one person who didn't think breast-feeding was painful, at least in the beginning.

Don't worry though. The pain subsides in a few months. If you're breast-feeding six times a day, that's only like 540 times before your boobs take on a shocked numb state.

Beyond the pain, there's also the uncertainty that your baby is actually drinking anything. If boobs were clear and you could actually see the milk draining from your body into your baby's, it would be easier to gain a level of confidence. But they are not and you have to trust your maternal instinct, which is tough when you're like me and you don't really have one.

I ended up hiring a doula who was a lactation specialist to come to my house for a few hours the first week to help make sure I was doing it right. She helped my positioning, told me to throw out my nipple shields, taught me the frozen cabbage trick (google it), and assured me Mazzy was getting her fill. That was invaluable.

Good things never come easy, and in my mind, breast-feeding is one of those things. You have to put in your time with the gnashing and the bleeding nipples. Once I got it down though, I really did enjoy it. And now that I've got bigger kids who won't stop moving, cuddling skin to skin in a glider chair for fifteen minutes every couple hours sounds like a dream.

Equal Partners, My Ass

Prior to having a baby, my husband and I prided ourselves on an equal partnership. We both worked, brought in similar incomes, and had the same schedule. Even though I was planning to go back to work after my maternity leave, having a baby created a whole new disparity that I wasn't expecting. Please take a look at the chart on the next page to see a side-by-side comparison of the tasks assigned to me and my husband during the newborn stage.

I mean, I'm sure Mike thought about us every now and again while checking email and drinking coffee uninterrupted, but I couldn't help but be a bit jealous.

At the end of the day, Mike would waltz in ("Hi, honey, I'm home!") like he had just spent a day at the spa, all excited to see the baby because, DUH—he'd spent the past nine hours without her, and suddenly everything we'd ever said about being equal partners seemed totally off the mark.

He also did this thing where he had to take off his coat, go to the bathroom, and "get settled," instead of removing the baby directly from my arms so I could get a break the second he walked in the door.

Even when Mike was around, it was totally uneven, because he just didn't have as much experience being with the baby. A simple task like changing Mazzy into a onesie would take him five times the time it would take me. Half the time would be spent asking me what he should put on her when there were clearly five million viable options in the drawer. JUST CHOOSE ONE. And then . . . the snaps would be all wrong. He couldn't breast-feed. Obviously. And his reaction time was too slow. Cries would wake me up in the middle of the night like the captain of the *Titanic* had just screamed, "ICEBERG!!!!" Whereas Mike would sleep right through it.

I realize now, it was unrealistic to expect Mike and me to take on equal responsibilities while I was on maternity leave, because my entire life revolved around the baby while he still had to show up for his job. Also, the two of us are just wired differently around a newborn. Mike took breaks, opted out of certain tasks (mainly because he couldn't lactate), and felt less guilty for leaving the house to take a walk, while I felt like my mom credentials would have been compromised if I allowed myself to step away from the baby for a second.

As our kids got older, our roles became a lot more equal. Mike turned out to be an awesome dad and way more responsible for the household than I ever expected (he cooks! he cleans!).

DISTRIBUTION OF NEWBORN RESPONSIBILITY

ME ⤭ MIKE

Breast-feeding around the clock	Who the hell knows, as he was at work living his previous life like nothing had happened.
Recording every pee and poop in a poop journal	
Desperately trying to implement a nap schedule	
Researching pediatricians (because the guy we chose who promised he was nowhere near retiring, totally retired)	
Organizing the baby room	
Trying and failing to shower	
Catching spit-up in my hand	
Changing and bathing the baby	
Doing more laundry than I ever thought possible	

So don't get divorced because your partner can't locate and clean a pacifier as quickly as you can.

I mean, he was always an awesome dad and husband. It just wasn't as obvious during the newborn phase.

So don't get divorced because your partner can't locate and clean a pacifier as quickly as you can. Or throw him under the bus in a tell-all (oops). Instead, wait a few years. It will probably even out in the long run.

So Much Gross

I can't think of many things that are both adorable and disgusting at the same time, but that is exactly what just popped out of your vagina. A pooping, belching, puking, drooling creature with a killer smile.

I'll keep this short because I don't want to write about all the horrid things that come out of a baby with acid reflux, just as much as you don't want to read about them. I've lived it. THAT'S ENOUGH.

I will tell you that, during the first year of my baby's life, the snot sucker became my best mom friend, and baby wipes were used for a million things beyond just wiping my baby.

Mazzy has a nose that runs with more urgency than Niagara Falls. I don't think I left the house once without dried-up snot on my shoulder for about three years. Harlow threw up everything she put in her mouth for the first six months. Her puke inspired me to come up with an invention that was basically burp cloths sewn into mittens. These would let you wipe up spit or catch puke without accidentally getting it on your hands. If you patent them, I GET A CUT.

Have I mentioned diaper blowouts? I'm going to save this important topic for it's very own chapter, but I will say this: When you leave the house with your newborn, PACK AN EXTRA SET OF CLOTHES (or three.)

I DON'T ALWAYS BLOW OUT MY DIAPERS BUT WHEN I DO, I MAKE SURE I AM FAR AWAY FROM HOME.

Making Your First Mom Friend

One odd component of new motherhood is the desperate need to make fast friends with other new mothers. And by other new mothers, I mean mothers whose children were born within a week of yours. Someone with a one-month-old? YOU WON'T RELATE TO THAT PERSON AT ALL. Time passes slowly for new moms.

Many women I know with older children made some of their best friends by joining a "new mommy" class and recommended this experience highly.

"There's an irreplaceable bonding that happens between new mothers. Trust me, you will make lifelong friends!" they said.

Lifelong friends??? That's a lot of pressure when you have limited time before you are heading back to the office. My closest friends and I have steadily built trust over the past twenty years. Banging out a BFF in a forty-minute class at the YMCA sounds like an unreasonable expectation.

But I was determined to give it my best shot!

At my first "new mommy" class, I remember entering the room and surveying my options. The room was set up with mats on the floor so that everyone would sit in a circle, but I was only the third person there, and the other two people were sitting on opposite sides. Which mom looked like she could be my next best friend? Surely you need to have the good fortune of sitting next to her on the very first day for the "irreplaceable bonding" to really take hold. What if my new best friend hadn't gotten there yet? Should I leave and come back when the class was more full? No, that would be weird. Should I just pick one and sit down? No, that seemed insulting to the other person.

So what did I do?

I opted to sit equidistant from both of them, aka next to no one. Immediately after I sat down, I realized my mistake. Now every other mother entering the room was judging me against the other two. Did I look like I had best-friend potential??

You know who finally sat down next to me? A freakin' dude. I mean, it's great there are new dads in the "new mommy" class, but I don't think my husband would like it if this guy was suddenly my new best friend.

New dad told me he managed a restaurant downtown so he worked at night. I told him my nipples felt like they were going to fall off and I hadn't pooped since I gave birth, but thanks for playing.

Once everyone was seated, I looked around the room to assess my baby's cuteness factor in relation to all the other babies. If any new mom tries to tell you that they do anything else when they meet a group of other new moms, THEY ARE LYING.

They also notice whose baby is holding their head up and which baby has the most hair and who is already wearing non-maternity clothes. Comparison is the evil side of "new mommy" class.

I also noticed the various blankets each mom (plus one dad) had set up for their babies to lie on. There were plush chenille blankets lined with satin, colorful modern blankets with graphic patterns, quilted pink blankets with ruffled edges, boyish blue blankets with truck or train motifs

> I told him my nipples felt like they were going to fall off and I hadn't pooped since I gave birth, but thanks for playing.

and sunny yellow gender-neutral blankets all spread out with care before their pride and joy was placed at its center.

It was clear the blanket setup said a lot about who you were as a parent and what kind of child you were raising.

Of course, I didn't realize you were supposed to bring a blanket and all I had was the generic receiving blanket I had gotten for free from the hospital. This blanket says one of two things: 1) I was an unpretentious parent who was taking a stand against overblown consumerism, or 2) I was a cheap bastard who didn't really love my baby.

I don't know if it was the blanket that sealed my fate or the fact that I sat next to a dad, but I did not make any lifelong friends in "new mommy" class.

However, I did get our dessert comped the first time Mike and I brought Mazzy out to a restaurant.

"Who is that guy?" my husband asked when the manager told us dessert was on him.

"My only friend from mommy class."

How To Take Advantage Of The Newborn Phase

When you're a newbie parent, every decision (even the ones that involve socks and washcloths) seems like the difference between life and death.

Once you have a second kid, you realize newborns are WAY easier than children at any other age. Unfortunately, at that point, you also have a toddler or a preschooler or a preteen or whatever and don't have the luxury of relaxing one-on-one with your small, sleepy, immobile, highly portable brand-new baby.

Hindsight is an interesting thing, and if I could do my first child over, I would totally find ways to take advantage of those first few months.

And no, I'm not going to say, "Sleep when the baby sleeps." I always found that to be a total crock.

1. FIND A MOM MENTOR.

The first time I walked into a Buy Buy Baby, I saw the wall of five thousand breast pump parts, almost had a panic attack, and walked right back out. Then I called a friend and said, "You tell me what I absolutely need and what brands worked for you, because I have no basis to make these decisions myself." She sent me her list and I bought whatever she said, without doing any research whatsoever. One mom you trust is way better than five hundred conflicting reviews on a random BabyCenter message board. And a lot less time consuming, too.

2. TAKE YOUR TIME.

Parents-to-be tend to go overboard preparing for the arrival of their baby, like all is lost if the nursery isn't fully set up on day one. But this isn't 1985, when you physically have to go to a furniture store to buy a changing table. Today you can buy everything online at home while sitting in your pajamas. Most babies sleep in their parents' room the first few months so . . . unless you're setting up the nursery as the perfect ending for your time-lapse-video birth announcement (which I totally support), you have plenty of time to buy and put together a crib after you come home from the hospital.

3. SAVE YOUR MONEY.

Stop buying so many zero-to-three-month clothes! I know it's hard because teeny-tiny Converse sneakers and newborn-sized faux fur jackets are adorable, but I promise—they won't ever make it out of the closet. It will take you about two days of ruining your baby's fancy French layette items before you switch to a steady diet of washable onesies and pajamas that come six in a pack. Also, all your friends and family members are going to inundate you with zero-to-six-month clothes. And then once your baby hits nine months, she'll have NOTHING. Nine-to-twelve-month clothes—that's what you should spend your money on.

4. BINGE-WATCH SHOWS ON NETFLIX.

Binge-watching a whole season of a show on a rainy, lazy Saturday is one of the main things I miss about my life before children.

Obviously, most shows worth watching are not toddler-appropriate, but when you have a newborn, all they see and hear are light and sounds. They won't really see the sexually explicit scenes in *Orange Is the New Black* any more than they'll learn how to make crystal meth by watching *Breaking Bad*. It's all good. If your baby is keeping you up in the middle of the night or perfectly content staring up at the ceiling fan during the day, throw on a show and make that time worth everybody's while.

5. GO ANYWHERE AND EVERYWHERE.

Don't bother yourself with a stroller. Strollers make new moms freak out at every stairway and curb. They don't fit through the doors to your favorite coffee shop or allow you enough room to browse the sale racks at J.Crew. I suggest strapping that ten to fifteen pounds on your chest and wandering your neighborhood with complete freedom. Not only will you be able to go anywhere you want, your baby will be happy as a bird. Most likely napping, too. You can go shopping, walk around a museum, or take a stroll just because it's a nice day and, for once in your life, **YOU HAVE NOWHERE ELSE TO BE.**

6. WEAR THAT CARRIER AT HOME, TOO.

Babies want to be held all the time and do this annoying thing called "crying" every time you put them down. So how do you cook yourself a meal? Unload the dishwasher? Do a load of laundry? You strap that baby to your body so you have both hands free, just like you would if you left the house. I think my baby lived in my carrier for four solid months.

7. BRUNCH WITH YOUR FRIENDS.

Remember before you had kids, how you'd see people sitting in sidewalk cafés at ten a.m. on a Tuesday and think, *WHO ARE THESE PEOPLE??? Don't they have JOBS?!* Maternity leave is one of the few excuses in your life to have breakfast at a restaurant on a weekday. I'd skip the baby-wearing on these occasions and take your baby for a ride in the stroller right around nap time. If your baby goes down and your pancakes arrive right at about the same time, well, then you have struck MATERNITY-LEAVE GOLD.

8. DON'T STRESS OVER THE BABY WEIGHT YET.

Pregnancy is a great excuse to quit your diet, especially since most of us think it will only be a nine-month hiatus. In reality, after I gave birth, I found myself hungrier than ever, due to the milk-sucking machine attached to my boobs whose main purpose in life (besides love and devotion) was stealing my sustenance. Listen. Unless you are a B-list celebrity, you don't have to debut your bikini body on the cover of *US Weekly* one month after you give birth. Feel free to keep your maternity jeans in regular rotation for a little while—those jeans are AMAZING. I still pull mine out on occasion and I haven't been pregnant in over three years.

9. KISS YOUR DOCTOR.

Your doctor will tell you many things at your first post-birth visit, but you will only hear two of them—no exercise and no sex. Well, isn't that upsetting. Can she also write "No housework" on a piece of paper and tell my husband he is medically obligated to give me foot massages every night? Because that would be like HEAVEN ON EARTH. Also, if you want to pretend your doctor said you *still* weren't 100 percent healed after your six-week visit, nobody is reporting back to your spouse but you. Doctor-patient confidentiality is a beautiful thing.

10. GET CREATIVE!

There are few times in your life when you have a tiny adorable newborn at your disposal. She can't move, she sleeps often, and you are home alone most of the time. Are you a creative person? I've got some ideas for you.

Photoshop your baby doing extreme sports.

Position that baby on the floor and then craft insanely intricate surroundings during nap time. →

← *Put that baby in a business suit made for a full-grown man.*

Most important, hug that little thing like there's no tomorrow. She grows up fast.

I know, you hate when people say that. I do, too.

CHAPTER 4

Unsolicited Advice

What is it about having a baby that gives all strangers the right to act like your mother? Don't they know most of us have our own mothers to deal with?

Unsolicited parenting advice seems to come from everybody—strangers, relatives, neighbors, people standing behind you on line at the supermarket. From extreme opinions on your baby-name choice to issues with your baby's lack of mittens. WHY ARE STRANGERS SO FOCUSED ON MITTENS??? Don't they realize all babies find a way to tear those suckers off??

It starts when you are pregnant. I remember walking through a Food Fair and stopping to try a free taste of salami on a toothpick—a chunk about the size of a pebble. The guy manning the salami must have been around seventeen. "I'm sorry, ma'am. I can't give this to you," he said while eyeing my belly up and down. Looking back, he was probably just trying to educate me on something he thought I didn't know (cured meat is not recommended for consumption by pregnant women), but it didn't matter, I felt embarrassed and wanted to scratch his eyes out.

people were being nearly as judgmental as it felt at the time, but I was really insecure and felt like everything was a personal attack even if someone was merely trying to offer some advice.

How do I know this? Because now that my kids are three and six, I want to offer new moms advice all the time. Not because I'm judging them, but because there are things I wish I knew then that I know now. If only someone had taken the time to tell me. . . .

Oh wait, they probably did but I didn't want to listen.

I CALL IT NEW MOM INSECURITY SYNDROME, AND HERE'S HOW YOU KNOW THAT YOU HAVE IT:

★ **When someone offers to help you, you think they are implying you can't do it yourself.**

★ **When someone says, "I think your baby pooped," you hear "A good mother would have noticed before I did."**

★ **When someone says, "It's cold outside. You should get your baby a hat," you hear "It will be a miracle if your baby survives the week."**

★ **When someone seems surprised that you're going back to work, you hear "How sad that someone else will raise your child."**

One time, I was taking a five-month-old Mazzy on a plane. I was holding her as we stood in line to board and she was sucking on a pacifier. The man behind me said, "Let me do you a favor and throw that dummy in the trash."

I was speechless. And shaking. I remember wanting to cry and knowing this was the absolute worst way to begin a cross-country flight with a baby. If I had my wits about me, I would have said, "Sure! And then you can sit with my wailing infant on your lap for the next six hours on the plane!"

Here's the thing: Being a new mom is a very vulnerable thing to be. Looking back, I don't think

★ **When someone seems surprised that you are staying at home, you hear "How sad that you lost all your ambition."**

New moms can't win. But seasoned moms trying to offer a little hard-earned advice can't win, either.

Accepting Help

Let me tell you a little story about my mother.

After Mazzy was born, my mother was around nonstop. She was there to change a diaper, to make me a meal, to suggest a shower, and to put on Mazzy's socks because "Oh my god! Her feet are freezing!"

After a few weeks, "Oh my god! Her feet are freezing!" began to sound like Grammy code for "Let me take care of your baby because you obviously have no idea what you're doing."

It was true. I had no idea what I was doing. But I also felt this need to show my mom I was capable, and so I got annoyed with her whenever she was trying to help.

"Let me collapse the stroller."

"No, I can do it."

"I'll give Mazzy a bath."

"That's not necessary."

"Why don't I watch Mazzy while you take a walk and get some air?"

"No, Mom. I'm fine."

My mother's extreme helpfulness seemed like a covert agenda to ensure my baby chose her in a custody battle one day.

After a solid month of shunning my mother's support, my mom broke down and got

That's my mom. (AKA Grammy)

understandably upset. We talked and I realized she was trying to make herself indispensable because she wanted to be around her grandchild more, not because she doubted my ability to parent.

Once I dropped my own insecurities out of the equation, accepting my mother's help was the very best thing. Why did I feel the need to do everything? Of course you can change her diaper. And, yes, by all means, give her a bath. While you're at it, I'm going out to buy some ice cream and get a pedicure.

Just be forewarned: Six years later, my kids would totally choose Grammy in a custody battle.

I'm okay with that, though.

10 QUESTIONS TO ASK YOURSELF BEFORE YOU ASK A WOMAN "WHEN ARE YOU DUE?"

Hollywood would have you believe that every woman's belly immediately deflates after giving birth. So it can be somewhat upsetting for a new mom when she leaves the hospital still looking very much pregnant. This is one reason why you should never ask a woman "when are you due?" If you are thinking about asking this question, here are some questions to ask yourself first.

1 Did she just tell you she is pregnant and you are asking a follow-up question?

2 Does she have a baby actively coming out of her vagina?

3 Are you an HR person fielding questions about when she will be on maternity leave?

4 Did she just throw up on your shoes and say, "GODDAMN MORNING SICKNESS!"?

5 Is she standing on line at the drugstore holding a baby-naming book and a tube of hemorrhoid cream?

6 Are you the receptionist checking her in for her OB appointment?

7 Is she sitting next to you in lamaze class?

8 Did she just inhale a boatload of food and say "Eating for two!"?

9 Did her water just break on the floor in front of you?

10 Did she just say "I am pregnant"?

If you answered "yes" to five or more of the above questions, YOU STILL NEVER ASK A WOMAN IF SHE IS PREGNANT. Even if you answered "yes" to #10, you may have misheard her.

Oh My, What Big Hair You Have!

When strangers aren't offering up unwanted parenting advice, they like to comment on your new baby's absurdly large ears, ridiculously chubby cheeks, or her spot-on resemblance to Danny Devito. "Those ears are way too large for that little head!" someone commented about Mazzy. "She looks like one of those troll dolls everyone collected in the 90s!" someone offered about Harlow's gravity-defying hair. My mom kept clipping little barrettes to get Harlow's locks to stay down. But you know what? I loved her epic head of baby hair. I say don't just embrace it. Name it.

THE SYDNEY OPERA HOUSE

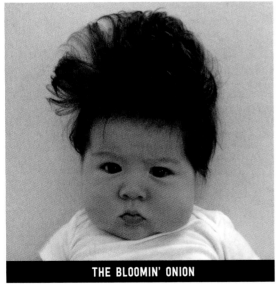

THE BLOOMIN' ONION

THE SCRIBBLE

THE GOLDFISH

THE JERSEY MOBSTER

THE BENJAMIN FRANKLIN

THE DONALD TRUMP IN A WINDSTORM

CHAPTER 5

Holy Crap, I'm Tired

You've heard about the lack of sleep. You imagined what it might be like. But nothing truly prepares you for the CRUSHING EXHAUSTION of parenthood until you actually experience it for yourself. It really puts celebrity hospitalizations "for exhaustion" into perspective. Lying in bed, watching TV, while someone delivers you Jell-O? Sounds like vacation! Maybe Lindsay Lohan was onto something.

Parenthood exhaustion is not like when you stayed up all night to study for a final in college. Or when you went out partying until five a.m. and then paid for it the next morning. In both those instances, do you remember what you did the next day?

YOU MADE UP FOR THE SLEEP.

You slept late, you took it easy for the day, and then you went to bed early. You did that as often as possible until you were back on track.

When you're a parent, there is no making up for lost sleep. You simply must survive on whatever time you are given. Which is not much. Especially when you have a newborn who parties every night like it's 1999 and then wakes up ridiculously early, too.

They say an hour nap in the middle of the day is equal to three hours of sleep at night. I think three hours of sleep in a glider chair is equal to about fifteen minutes of sleeping in a bed. Even so, "glider chair sleep" might be the only sleep you get, so FOR THE LOVE OF GOD, make sure you purchase a comfortable rocker. I wanted to get one of those Eames molded-plastic rockers that were all the rage when Mazzy was born. *We'd have the perfect hipster nursery with that rocker!*

Mike (my very practical husband who is SO NOT A HIPSTER) took one look at the Eames rocker and said, "No way. You're not going to want to breast-feed the baby in the middle of the night in that thing." I conceded, even though it pained me to do so (my modern chic nursery dreams dashed!), but a few nights into motherhood, I realized that buying a comfy glider chair was one of the best decisions we made.

Here's my advice: Shop for a rocker like you shop for a new mattress, because that will be your bed. I slept in that thing up until we got rid of it when Mazzy turned five.

HIPSTER ROCKER vs COMFY GLIDER

HIPSTER ROCKER

Looks good in photos when your nursery is featured on Apartment Therapy

COMFY GLIDER

Is something you actually want to sit in every night at 3 a.m.

Early Rising

Six a.m. seems like a reasonable time to wake up—still early, but clearly morning. Unfortunately, my babies both liked to wake up around five thirty a.m., when I could barely function. I'm sure a half hour doesn't sound like much to most people, but for me it's the difference between a functioning brain and something closer to mush.

Me at six a.m.: I hop out of bed, ready to start the day!

Me at five thirty a.m.: I stumble out of bed, get my foot caught in the sheets, and smash my face into the ground.

Parenthood is otherworldly exhaustion.

Seriously, I can't think of one thing more exhausting than having a newborn.

Wait. "Mom Brain" Is A Real Thing?

There is a reason new moms are encouraged to keep a journal of every pee and poop. There are also watches that will tell you which boob you used to breast-feed last. Thermometers that work with your phone to tell your doctor when your child has a temperature. The reason is because you will not remember otherwise.

Before I had a baby, I had the power to memorize ATM card pin numbers and the birthdays of my closest friends. After I had a baby (particularly in the first few months), if you told me, **"The bottle is on the kitchen counter,"** and the bottle was in fact on the kitchen counter, I would still

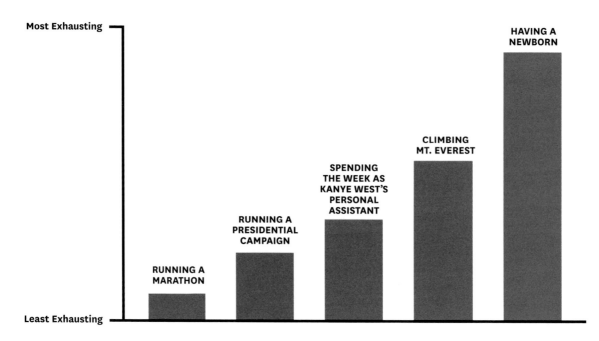

not be able to find it. If I needed to pack an overnight bag, I would forget at least three items. Not minor items, mind you—I would forget diapers, clothes for myself, and the breast pump. And if you asked me to locate my keys in a bag with only two other items, it would still take me at least fifteen minutes to find them.

I've been known to freak out because I can't find my phone WHILE I AM ON THE PHONE. This happens to me all the time. The best part is—I tell the person I'm on the phone with, "Shit! I can't find my phone!" And they're like, "Oh no! Where did you last see it?" Because the person I am on the phone with is most likely a mom as well and can't put two and two together, either.

This is a phenomenon called Mom Brain. And if you must know, I spelled that "Mom Brian" before I went back and corrected it.

What is Mom Brain? When you have a baby, your thought process becomes so consumed with the all-important task of keeping another human being alive that everything less important gets relegated to the back of your brain.

That ATM card pin number I spoke about earlier? I had owned the same card with the same pin number for the past ten years, and after I had a baby, the number just left my head. Flew straight out with no advance warning. One day I was getting money from the bank, the next day I was standing there staring blankly at the keypad, blinking like a cartoon character with birds flying inside her brain. I kept going back to the bank, thinking another visit to the ATM would activate my long-term memory. Nope. I had to get a new card with a new pin.

This time, I wrote that shit down. Where? I have no idea.

Shirking Nighttime Responsibilities 101
(LESSONS LEARNED FROM MY HUSBAND)

While Mike didn't have Mom Brain, he had another problem: He cannot function on less than eight hours of sleep. In fact, the mere act of me waking up next to him to tend to our baby was enough of a disruption to render him useless the following day.

At first I accepted this, but after a few months of tending to our baby in the middle of the night on my own, I came to believe he had devised several strategies that allowed him a full night's sleep.

STRATEGY #1:
FEIGNING BEDTIME INEPTITUDE
The more I put the baby to sleep, the less accustomed the baby was to having Mike around during bedtime. I believe Mike's goal was to make his mere presence upset "The Bedtime Routine" so supremely that it was easier for everyone if he was left out of the process. I was more used to handling bedtime anyway, since I was nursing the baby to sleep during the first few months. The longer I nursed, the easier it was for Mike to pretend he had no place in the routine. When I stopped nursing, I thought Mike had no excuse but to take some responsibility at night. This is when he employed his next big strategy.

STRATEGY #2:
OPERATION BEDTIME FAIL
Eventually, Mike agreed to put the baby to bed. He went in the nursery with her and shut the door, giving me no window into what was going on in there. This I believe was a key part

of his strategy. Mazzy always cried when I put her down, but at least I knew exactly what was happening. With the door shut and Mike on the inside, I could let my imagination run wild. For all I knew, Mike did absolutely nothing to calm Mazzy, just waited the appropriate amount of time and then emerged from the nursery with mussed hair and a frazzled face, still awkwardly holding a very wide-awake baby. Kind of like that old Rice Krispies commercial where the woman

purposefully throws flour on her face before opening the kitchen door with her Rice Krispies treats. Then Mike would present my bleary-eyed baby to me, claiming, "It's not working." Of course, at this point, I just opted to do it myself. It's one thing to make your husband participate. It's another to do it at the expense of the baby. Mike made sure to have the worst bedtime track record imaginable so that eventually I only asked for his help in absolute emergencies.

STRATEGY #3: BABY MONITOR CHICKEN

Mike established early on that he sleeps like a rock. Nothing wakes him up—not thunder, not sirens, not naked, screaming women streaking through the room. His "hard to wake" credentials were firmly in place by the time we had our baby, so it was not a surprise when he did not wake on his own when our baby cried in the middle of the night. Whether this was all an act that he started while we were dating just so he could employ it later on, I have no idea. It's possible. He's a pretty smart guy. Maybe the baby did wake him up but he just pretended otherwise and I never questioned him. That is possible, too. Even when I tried to wake him up, he wouldn't wake up. We're talking physically shaking and smacking his body and still nothing. It almost seemed impossible. Like his goal was to make the act of waking him up harder than the act of just tending to the baby myself.

STRATEGY #4: BEAR ATTACK

Eventually, I resorted to extreme measures of waking him—shouting, hitting, nudity, etc. It was at this point that Mike employed an "unfavorable wake-up demeanor." It was not angry. More fearful. Like, imagine how someone would react if they woke up to a bear attacking them in their tent. FYI, an over-the-top body shudder combined with a look of sheer terror works brilliantly to deter someone from waking you from your peaceful slumber.

STRATEGY #5: CHICKEN WITHOUT A HEAD

At a certain point, I was prepared to stop at nothing to get my husband out of bed and for him to recognize that "his turn" was long overdue. It was then that Mike deployed his trump card: the last trick up his sleeve. He jumped out of bed like a crazy person, looked wildly around the room to get his bearings, and shouted in a totally deranged tone of voice, "Okay! It's my turn to get the baby!" Then he ran straight into a wall. The beauty of this technique is that, even though I was about to lose my mind at the thought of one more sleepless night, I was not about to entrust my baby in the arms of someone who just ran into a wall.

Clever, right? What a dad will do to get some sleep.

The Schmucks & The Schmugaboo: A Cautionary Tale

Parental Exhaustion and Mom Brain will affect your life in numerous small ways, but for us, there was one major event that really drove our lack of clear thinking home. This super-embarrassing story revolves around the purchase of a stroller. Did I say this was our story? Mike and I would never do anything this dumb. This story is about another couple we know. Their names are Schilana and Schmike.

Schilana and Schmike live in New York City. In New York City in 2009, if you gave birth to a baby, you most likely bought a Bugaboo stroller. As the Mercedes of baby strollers, it was priced at approximately $1,000.

I know, EXPENSIVE.

But Schilana wanted a Bugaboo very badly. Not only was she told they were the best strollers for handling rough city terrain, but they came in cool

Schilana looked up pictures of the Bugaboo online and determined that their Bugaboo didn't look nearly as nice as advertised.

colors and all her friends had them. Schmike, on the other hand, thought paying $1,000 for a stroller was obscene. But when Schilana sets her mind to attaining something she deems necessary, especially if it is for the good of their brand-new baby, it is next to impossible to sway her.

Schilana was not entirely unreasonable though. When she found out some of her friends had bought used Bugaboos on Craigslist, she decided to check it out. She ended up doing one better.

Schilana found a woman who had three brand-new Bugaboos, one even in the color she was coveting. The woman said that her boyfriend worked for a company where they sold overstock. Each Bugaboo was in its original box, packed with the instruction manual and the user DVD, and cost $600. Schilana, feeling bolder than usual, suggested $500. They settled on $550. Schmike would be so pleased!

Schilana and Schmike arranged to meet the woman at her apartment uptown. Schilana asked for her apartment number. The woman said she would meet them with the stroller in the lobby. Which was understandable. Why

give strangers your apartment number if it wasn't neccessary?

When Schilana and Schmike arrived at the building, the woman arrived shortly after by walking in the front door and lugging the box inside. Which was odd. But then she explained that since their apartment was small, they kept the strollers in their car. Okay, that made sense.

Being a smart guy, Schmike checked out the contents of the box before finalizing the deal. Inside, all the Bugaboo pieces appeared to be new and accounted for. Complete with the instruction manual and user DVD as advertised. Schmike handed the woman a check. She said she didn't take checks. So Schilana waited with the woman while Schmike went to a bank to take out $550 in cash.

Then Schmike and Schilana went home, proud of their resourcefulness, their frugality, and most of all, their brand-new Bugaboo!

Once home, Schmike went about the task of assembling the Bugaboo. He struggled with the fabric. It pulled in some areas and sagged in others. Schilana looked up pictures of the Bugaboo online and determined that their Bugaboo didn't look nearly as nice as advertised.

Then the time came for Schmike and Schilana to take the baby out for a stroll. To proudly pull up their Bugaboo next to all the other Bugaboos at the playground. But as they rolled the stroller outside, the front wheel started to squeak. A block later, they noticed the baby was rolling to one side of the bassinet. They rolled her back. She rolled again. The bassinet appeared to be tilted, so they quickly retreated back to their apartment.

Once home, Schmike called the Bugaboo customer service line for advice. (I'm improvising

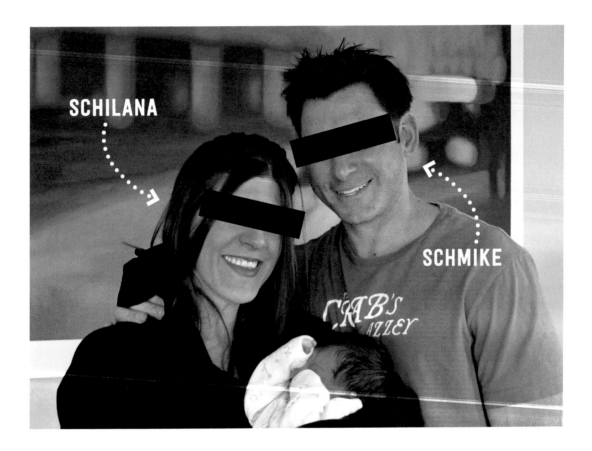

SCHILANA

SCHMIKE

now, because of course Shilana and Schmike are just friends of mine and there is no way for me to know everything word for word, but . . .) The conversation went something like this:

"I'm experiencing difficulties putting together my stroller."

"Can you please tell me the product code of the stroller?"

"Where would that be?"

"On the bottom of the frame."

"I don't see any code."

"It is right in the middle on the bottom."

"I still don't see anything."

"What about the box? Is there a sticker on it?"

"No."

And then the agent said the most awful sentence in history:

"It appears you have purchased a fake Bugaboo." GASP!!!!!!!

Schmike and Schilana reflected. They thought about how the woman was offering three brand-new strollers at half the price, how easily Schilana had bargained with her, the secretive nature of the apartment number, the trunk full of strollers parked outside the building, the rejection of the check and the subsequent trip to the bank . . . and it all seemed glaringly obvious. Or it would have been glaringly obvious if they hadn't recently been all consumed with their newborn.

In the end, they salvaged the frame and bought all new Bugaboo parts. The fabric had the perfect amount of tautness, the bassinet lay flat, the wheels handled with squeakless precision, and it looked just as perfect as the Bugaboos on the company website.

Grand total for the fake Bugaboo plus the real Bugaboo parts? $1,000.

To their friends and everyone they passed on the street, Schilana and Schmike owned a $1,000 Bugaboo.

But secretly, Schilana and Schmike knew that they were the schmucks with a $1,000 Schmugaboo.

How To Deal With Exhaustion

So what to do? How do you cope with crippling exhaustion and the brain of a flea without making ridiculously bad purchase decisions?

God, I don't know. I'm still wondering how I'm supposed to get two kids up and ready for school and make it out myself in a semi-presentable fashion.

In the beginning, I say—don't try to do too much. Just concentrate on your baby.

Have a big heaping cup of coffee and toast your new level of exhaustion with a little Baby Mugging.

What Is Baby Mugging?

Good question! Baby Mugging is holding a mug in front of your baby, so that it completely obscures their body and snapping a photo so that it creates the illusion your baby's head is popping out of your mug. That's it. No Photoshop necessary.

★ **Step 1) Put your baby on the floor.**

★ **Step 2) Hold a mug in front of your baby.**

★ **Step 3) Take a photo.**

★ **Step 4) Finish your coffee.**

CHAPTER 6

All Maternity Leaves Must Come To An End

Are you a stay-at-home mom? You might want to skip this chapter. This chapter is for moms going back to work—the reluctant-to-return and the I CAN'T WAIT TO TALK TO ADULTS ABOUT THINGS OTHER THAN DIAPER DUTIES kind of moms. I am the latter, FYI. Doesn't mean I love my kids any less.

Or does it?

Oh, working mom guilt. We'll talk about that, too.

This chapter will cover entrusting your mini-me in the hands of a complete stranger, navigating work as a mom (You want me to stay late for a six p.m. meeting? ARE YOU INSANE???), and all that time you'll spend in the "lactation room."

But first let's start with prepping for your return to work, which includes a once enjoyable task that is now prime fodder for your worst nightmares. That task is clothes shopping.

Did you just shudder? You must have recently had a baby.

You see, women have looked helplessly at their full closets of clothes since the beginning of time and claimed, "I have nothing to wear." But when you are heading back to work with a deflated basketball in place of your belly, this is actually true.

Post-Maternity Clothes Shopping (A Play In Three Acts)

(ACT I)

SALES WOMAN: Can I help you?

NEW MOM: Yes, I'm looking for a pair of pants that are nice enough to wear out in public but not too nice that I'll be upset if my baby pukes on them. The fabric should be easily washable and wrinkle-resistant. They should sit high enough on my waist to make sure my butt crack doesn't show when I play on the floor, but low enough that they won't be mistaken for pants my mom would have worn in the eighties. They should be tight enough to hide my post-baby belly but not too tight that my belly rolls over the top. Most importantly, they need to be something basic that will not call attention to the fact I am wearing the same item of clothing over and over again.

SALES WOMAN: Might I interest you in a pair of yoga pants?

NEW MOM: I'm already wearing yoga pants.

SALES WOMAN: Then I can't help you.

(END SCENE)

―――――――――――――

(ACT II)

SALES WOMAN: Can I help you?

NEW MOM: Yes, I'm looking for a button-down shirt to make breast-feeding easy. But the fabric needs to have enough give so the buttons don't tug across my ginormous rack. The shirt should be long enough to cover the top of my ill-fitting pants and loose enough to hide what is going on underneath. Something with a pattern to camouflage stains but nothing so bold that people will notice I've been wearing the same shirt for the past five days. My bra straps need to be accessible, but not exposed, since they are about five inches thick and look like the bra straps more commonly worn by a senior citizen. Most importantly, the top needs to have no discernable waist since I am unsure when or if mine will ever return.

SALES WOMAN: Perhaps you should be looking in our pajama section.

NEW MOM: As I suspected.

(END SCENE)

―――――――――――――

(ACT III)

NEW DAD: I thought you went clothes shopping today.

NEW MOM: I did.

NEW DAD: But those look like the same clothes you've been wearing for the past two months.

NEW MOM: Get used to them because I will be wearing them for the next eighteen years.

(FINI)

―――――――――――――

Entrusting Your Baby To A Complete Stranger

The next step in going back to work is finding someone or somewhere to trust with your baby. We went the nanny route because I live in NYC and day care really isn't much less expensive. Plus, getting your kid into a good day care isn't easy. In fact, we applied to a reputable day care while I was pregnant and were put on the waiting list. We are *still* on that waiting list and my baby just turned six.

Finding the right nanny is a tough process because you barely trust yourself with your baby and here you are, taking a huge leap of faith on someone else. I have never Facebook-stalked so much in my life than when we were interviewing nannies. But instead of looking for pictures of guys with their previous girlfriends, I was looking for pictures of potential nannies with previous children.

Look, there's a picture of her with a baby! The baby looks like he really likes her! Wait. Do you think the baby likes her more than his own mom? Because that wouldn't be good . . .

Yes, that is the fear of every working mother. That you'll walk into your home and your child will cling to your nanny, devastated by your return.

To make yourself feel better, just remember the separation anxiety your baby experienced when you left in the morning. Those screams were **DEVASTATING.** Your baby loves you *that* much.

Pop Quiz! What's harder? Forcing your distressed baby into the arms of your nanny while she screams for her mommy? Or having your happy baby practically leap into the arms of your nanny the second she walks in the door?
Trick question. They are equally hard.

Obviously, you want the happy baby who grows to love her nanny. You want the competent caregiver who knows your baby's schedule better than you do. You just have to remind yourself that nannies are temporary and you will be there for the rest of your kid's life. Whether she wants you there or not.

Nobody replaces Mom.

Back At Work, Kind Of

Every new mom's experience going back to work is different. For instance, if I were a doctor actually saving lives, I think I might have felt less guilt about working late than as a Creative Director in advertising who was fielding emergency calls about the possibility of losing a cracker account (true story).

Or maybe all new moms back at work feel the same amount of guilt, no matter what they do. It's just this weird process of weighing what you're paid and what you do all day against time spent with your baby. And even though most of us need the paycheck, you may still feel guilty for actually enjoying the time away.

For me, being back at work was even more confusing because my company had made some big shifts in management while I was on maternity leave, and everyone I had worked for previously was gone with no one in their place. My first day back, an executive from the Chicago office called all the creative directors into a meeting to tell us they were in the process of looking for someone new.

"In the meantime, just continue managing your accounts," he said confidently.

I raised my hand. "Ummmm . . . What if it's your first day back from maternity leave and you were transitioned off all of your accounts?"

"That's a good question! You'll probably work your ass off trying to prove yourself to powers that literally aren't there, while spending half your time locked in a bathroom pumping milk into plastic bags and the other half of your time going to necessary well visits at the pediatrician while all your childless coworkers think you're making these appointments up to get out of work. Every time you stay late, you'll feel like a horrible mother and every time you leave early, you'll feel like a terrible team player at the office. Then a few months down the line, after you've taken your baby and your mother on a work trip so you can pretend you are just as capable and available as you were pre-baby, we'll let you go as part of a larger layoff initiative. Sound good?"

Well, he didn't really say that, but that's how it went down.

I had three months back at the office before the layoff and then I started freelancing at various agencies, lugging my breast pump all over Manhattan. I have seen more lactation rooms than most, and let me just say—most of them aren't good. If they exist at all.

The Pumping Life

The lactation room at my first office was a bathroom without a toilet in a weird corner of the building. You got to it via a random hallway that I never even knew existed during my thirteen years at the company. Inside was a shower stall next to a sink with a stool and an outlet. I sat on that stool in that tiny room two to three times a day, fifteen minutes at a time, hooked up to my pump while looking at cute pics of my baby on the phone, like a man looking at porn while he's trying to ejaculate in a cup. Then I'd disassemble the pieces, clean everything, get dressed, run out with my machinery in a "super-chic portable tote!" directly into a production meeting with my dress tucked into the back of my tights (yes, that happened) like— nothing weird to see here! Just a working mom multitasking!

The worst was when you'd get to the lactation room and someone else would already be locked inside. You had no idea if she was on minute one or minute fourteen, so sometimes your fifteen-minute pumping adventure would turn into a half-hour expedition. Once, I made the mistake of leaving and coming back only to find a third pumping mom waiting outside the door. At that point my boobs felt like they were going to explode and I never made that mistake again.

During the period while I was freelancing, I pumped in all different places. Smaller agencies didn't have a designated spot, so I would have to make it up as I went along. I've pumped in a stairwell, a restaurant bathroom, a utility closet, and a makeup trailer.

At one agency, my only option was to pump in a glass office. I took a large piece of foam core and sat it on a chair, leaning up against the glass, so that if anybody walked by, they wouldn't be able to see what I was doing. Then I locked the door and went about my business, while watching the tops of people's heads bobbing above the foam core as they passed by.

The foam core worked successfully for about four days and then, on the fifth day, God said, "LET THE FOAM CORE FALL, BECAUSE THAT WOULD BE HILARIOUS!" The board tipped over mid-pumping session but still blocked the bottom half of the window, so I just kind of shimmied off

my chair and onto the floor to finish the job.

That's one of those moments that you don't really imagine when you think about becoming a mom.

Why do we do it?

For me, pumping made me feel connected to my baby even though I wasn't there. It was a sacrifice that felt right to me if I was ever feeling particularly guilty about indulging my career. Which was often.

Some people hate the pump. I actually liked the relief of the letdown and the reminder that my life was different now. Plus, it was a very convenient time to read blogs, check email, sort through photos, and text my friends.

Yes, pumping is disruptive and not the most pleasant feeling in the world, but once you are hooked up, it's kind of a welcome break.

Except when a random guy walks in on you.

The Time A Man Walked In On Me While I Was Pumping At Work

Originally, I was going to write this story as "The Ten Phases Of A Male Coworker Walking In on You While You're Pumping," but I couldn't get past "Phase #1: Ohmygodohmygodohmygodohmygod . . ."

It was traumatizing. And not just for me— FOR THE GUY.

It was a young man, about twenty-five, who, prior to walking in on me, probably didn't even know breast pumps existed. When this man eventually has children of his own, I bet he recounts this story to his wife as the reason he cannot even bear to look at her hooked up to a pump. TOO MANY HORRIBLE MEMORIES.

First, just so you understand the exact scenario, I was freelancing at a production company and had been using their coed bathroom as my pumping room. It's one stall, so I would just lock the door. There's no counter, so I had to balance my pump on the sink and do my business standing up.

In this instance, as always, I took my shirt off. Unhooked those little clippies on my maternity bra. Put my strapless pumping bra on. You know, the really sexy nippleless bra with the yellow breast-milk stains on it. I assembled the pump, plugged it in, attached myself, etc., etc.

I did everything except (as I was about to learn) LOCK THE GODDAMN DOOR.

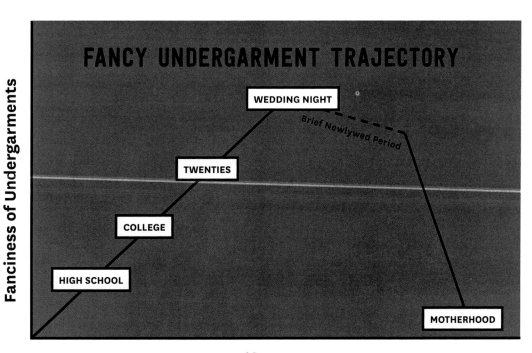

FANCY UNDERGARMENT TRAJECTORY

Fanciness of Undergarments

WEDDING NIGHT

Brief Newlywed Period

TWENTIES

COLLEGE

HIGH SCHOOL

MOTHERHOOD

Life Stage *

* This chart is for married women with children. If you go through life as a single woman or you never have any kids, I imagine the fanciness of your undergarments continues to increase until you are eventually killed by the weight of your own solid-gold brassiere.

Then the poor guy opens the door and sees me but doesn't really understand what's happening, so he just stands there paralyzed, staring at me while I scream internally, **_WHY AREN'T YOU MOVING??? GET THE FUCK OUT!!!!!!_**

A half second later (the longest half second in history), when he finally snapped to and started apologizing profusely (DON'T APOLOGIZE! GET THE FUCK OUT!!!!), my first instinct was to try to quickly slam the door in his face, but **1)** I was attached to the wall, so the sudden movement made the breast pump fall to the ground, and **2)** it turns out, it was one of those heavy metal doors that's impossible to slam because it has some sort of pressurized thing happening to ensure it closes slowly.

PICTURE THIS: 1) Door flung open to reveal me topless, hooked up to milk machine. **2)** Machine falls to ground, still attached to breasts. **3)** Despite pushing with all my might, door closes at speed of turtle.

MORTIFYING.

Luckily, since I was freelancing on a short-term project, I had never seen the guy who entered the bathroom before. I know he was wearing stripes and glasses, but I cannot picture his face. In my breast-pumping nightmares, Where's Waldo walks in on me. I'm hoping in his breast-pumping nightmares, he can picture tubes and nipples but he cannot summon my face, either.

KEEP OUT!

BOOBS AT THEIR UNSEXIEST INSIDE.

YOU KNOW YOU'RE A WORKING MOM IF . . .

1 You've poured out your purse in order to find a pen in a meeting and a pair of My Little Pony underpants fell out.

2 You've said, "I have to take my kid to the doctor" so many times, you're sure your boss thinks you are lying, even though it has been true every time.

3 You've spent half the day at the office before realizing you have an Elmo sticker stuck to the back of your shirt.

4 You have three sets of clothes: things I wear at home, things I wear out at night, and work clothes that allow me to pump in the lactation room without getting fully naked.

5 You know that closing the zipper compartment around the motor of your breast pump will make the pumping noise low enough for you to participate in a conference call.

6 You've infected your entire office with a preschool stomach virus.

7 At least one of your male coworkers has seen your breasts. And not due to a torrid office affair.

8 You've shouted into a phone in an open office full of people, "YOU POOPED IN THE POTTY??? THAT'S AMAZING!!!"

9 You've laughed at the 22-year-old junior employee when she complained about being "so tired" after one late night out. Amateur.

10 In addition to playing princesses and superheroes, your daughter plays "going to work," which consists of pretending to type on a computer while yelling, "I said, give me a second!"

11 You've felt guilty for leaving your kids on a particularly rough morning because you had to go to work.

12 You've felt guilty for leaving your team before a project was finished because you had to go home to see your kids.

13 You've thought numerous times about what it would be like to stay at home, but ultimately, whether it be because you love your work, you need the money, or you wouldn't be happy at home all day with the kids, you know this is the best decision for your family. As time goes on, you realize having a part of your life that is not wrapped up in your children is a good thing, and finding fulfillment at your job helps you feel sane at home.

MAJOR MILESTONES

CHAPTER 7

And You Thought *Your* Diet Was Hard

Eating is a basic function. Our favorite function. Often, our entire social life revolves around our need to eat. Which is why it's all the more confusing when our newborns struggle with this simple concept. Infants not only have a limited menu (milk only, please!), they make reservations at three a.m. when we'd rather be sleeping. They may choose the ease of the bottle over the comfort of Mom, which is downright insulting. Or they refuse the bottle and insist on Mom, meaning you are their indentured servant for the next year.

Once breast-feeding is over, it doesn't get any easier. That's when your kitchen floor will be regularly covered by smashed peas and pureed carrots. That's when they will make their INSANELY SPECIFIC banana preferences known. And their taste buds appear to be more fickle than that asshole from Sigma Nu who dated you and every one of your friends in college. And if you've ever parented a toddler, you know there is really only one thing they are guaranteed to eat: ketchup.

Yogurt On The Ceiling

You won't realize how easy the milk stage is until your pediatrician says your baby is ready for solids. "Really?" you'll ask incredulously. "Are you sure she won't choke?" The pediatrician is sure— she has done this before.

When Mazzy started eating solids, I worked out a nice system where I fed her reasonably sized spoonfuls straight to her mouth. No mess. With Harlow, she kept trying to grab the spoon away from me, so I kept moving it out of her reach and then attempting to feed her again. It didn't really occur to me that she was trying to feed herself because Mazzy did it much later. I thought she was just trying to derail my efforts.

Word to the Wise: If you hold on to a spoon too tightly and your baby ends up snatching it from you, that creates a much bigger mess than if you just let her have the damn spoon from the get-go.

I thought I'd solve my problem by giving her a spoon to play with while I got a second spoon to accomplish the feeding. Genius, right?

Nope. Harlow wanted that one, too.

Okay. So I'll just hold the cup of yogurt so she can dip her spoon in. She'll be eating herself, so that should suffice, right?

Nope. Harlow made it clear, through various grunts and shrieks, that she would prefer me to place the yogurt cup on the high-chair tray, slowly back away, and leave her to her own devices.

BUT WON'T SHE JUST KNOCK THE THING TO THE FLOOR AND CREATE A HUGE MESS?!

Yes, she will. I was not going to be the only parent to ever make it through babyhood without cleaning food off the floor. Or the ceiling. Or the counter. Or the couch.

Things You Should Know About Feeding Solids That You Won't Learn From Your Pediatrician

★ Keep all evidence of bottles, milk, boobs, formula, cows, etc., out of sight while you are feeding the baby solids. Even the slightest glimpse of a bra strap can derail your efforts entirely.

★ Don't bend down to pick food up off the floor while the baby still has food on his/her plate. Unless you like the idea of a vegetable-medley hat.

Suction cup bowls work for approximately two minutes before your baby silmultaneously summons up the strength and the brainpower to pry the thing off. Use that two minutes wisely and be on the alert.

★ Don't microwave the suction cup bowls. Whatever minimal suctioning ability they currently possess will be completely lost.

★ If you do microwave the suction cup bowls, don't tell your mother. She will lecture you endlessly about putting plastic in the microwave.

★ Try not to be too impressed when your child successfully uses her pincer grasp to pick up a Puff or a Cheerio. "SHE'S A GENIUS!!!! ALERT SOCIAL MEDIA!!!!!!" FYI, those things are designed so that they stick to your baby's fingers.

★ Never pretend to understand the fickle taste buds of a child. Example: I thought pasta

would be a no-brainer. A person would have to be crazy not to like pasta—it's universally delicious! Turns out my baby is a COMPLETE WACK JOB.

★ If it is on your plate, the baby will want it. Even if the baby's plate contains the exact same thing. Don't try to rationalize—IT'S A BABY. Sheesh.

★ Do not attempt to understand people who use cloth bibs that need to be thrown in the wash after each use as opposed to waterproof plastic bibs that can be easily wiped clean. They are crazy people and they probably don't like pasta.

★ The longer the baby has food in front of her, the more likely that food will work its way up past her eyebrows and into her hair.

★ Think your baby made a big mess at dinner? Don't worry, someone else's baby has made a bigger mess.

MY TODDLER'S DINNER

Ketchup

78%

22%

Whatever food
is supposed to
be eaten with
the ketchup

MY TWO-YEAR-OLD'S RULES
FOR EATING A BANANA

Feeding babies might be messy, but at least it's not the mindfuck that is feeding a toddler. I'd take a baby who spills his rice cereal on the floor to a toddler having a tantrum about a banana that's sliced wrong any day of the week.

My toddler has more rules and restrictions about bananas than the TSA has about air travel.

1 You must peel the banana halfway down and hand her the whole thing.

2 If the banana is peeled any less than halfway down, she will not accept it.

3 If the banana is peeled any more than halfway down, she will not accept it.

4 If anyone attempts to give her a banana without the peel, she will not accept it.

5 If there are any brown spots on the banana, she will not accept it.

6 If you try to cut off a brown spot, she will notice and not accept it.

7 If you try to turn the banana and hand it to her so that she will not notice the brown spot, she will be even more pissed that someone tried to trick her.

8 If there are any stringy things hanging off the banana, she will freak out until you remove them.

9 Once she eats the banana down to the peel, she will tell you she is finished and request a new banana.

10 Don't point out that there is still half a banana left, she is already aware.

11 Don't peel the banana farther and try to hand it back, that bottom half is dead to her.

12 All of these restrictions will not prevent her from requesting bananas daily. SHE LOVES BANANAS.

Eating At A Restaurant

For all the reasons previously mentioned (messiness, pickiness, etc.), taking your kids out to eat in a restaurant is not for the novices among us.

You must be prepared (translation: bring predinner snacks) and informed (make sure ahead of time that they serve chicken fingers) and able to ignore the annoyed looks of fellow restaurant patrons who are just trying to enjoy their meal. You have to be OK with eating your meal cold, if at all. You need to be able to make nice with the server even when they keep putting full drinks at the edge of the table, delivering food on plates the temperature of the sun, and offering ice cream in the middle of dinner to stop your child from crying.

I recommend handing them the following note at the beginning of the meal:

Dear Server,

Hi. We don't know each other. Yet. But my children will be under both your and my care for the next one to two hours.

How that goes is up to both of us.

I know I may seem like an asshole when I demand bread and water before I even sit down at the table, but everything I do and say from this point forward is strictly to ensure that we are in and out of here quickly and with as little ado as possible.

We are on the same team, you and I.
Got it?

Okay.

Now take my order and bring the check with the food.

Sincerely,
YOUR NAME HERE
P.S. I have moved the cutlery and the candle intentionally. Please don't move them back.

The Picky-Eaters Club

While specific banana-eating habits might be universal when it comes to kids, there are tons of other foods that pose extreme issues as well; it varies wildly from child to child.

I like to induct these kids into the Picky-Eaters Club. Here are a few of our current members.

HELLO, MY NAME IS SYDNEY AND I REACT TO AVOCADO LIKE MY MOTHER IS TRYING TO POISON ME.

HELLO, MY NAME IS LOLA AND I THINK CHEESE AND TORTILLAS ARE DELICIOUS BUT IF YOU MELT THEM TOGETHER AND CALL IT A QUESADILLA, I WON'T TOUCH IT.

HELLO, MY NAME IS JACK AND I WILL ONLY EAT ICE CREAM FROM THE SAMPLE CUP. DON'T TRY TO GIVE ME ONE OF THOSE BIG CUPS OF ICE CREAM BECAUSE THOSE ARE JUST TERRIBLE.

HELLO, MY NAME IS ASHTON. I DON'T EAT MEAT, UNLESS IT'S A HOT DOG SERVED COLD. FYI, YOU MUST CALL IT A COLD DOG BECAUSE IF YOU CALL IT A HOT DOG (EVEN IF IT IS SERVED COLD), I WON'T TOUCH IT.

HELLO, MY NAME IS HAZY AND I LOVE SMOOTHIES! I MEAN, I LOVE ASKING MY MOM TO MAKE SMOOTHIES, HEARING THE BLENDER AND THEN HAVING THEM SIT IN FRONT OF ME ON THE TABLE. BUT I ONLY TAKE ONE SMALL SIP EVERY TIME.

HELLO, MY NAME IS HOLDEN AND I LIKE TOMATO SAUCE UNLESS I FIND A PIECE OF ACTUAL TOMATO IN IT.

HELLO, MY NAME IS ELI AND I'M NOT HUNGRY UNLESS DADDY PRETENDS MY FOOD IS CRYING OUT "PLEASE DON'T EAT ME!" THEN I GOBBLE IT UP IMMEDIATELY BECAUSE I'M NOT JUST A PICKY EATER, I'M A TODDLER SOCIOPATH.

CHAPTER 8

Just Go To Bed Already

Sleep is probably the most talked about parenting topic. It's like new parents are so consumed with setting up a sleep schedule that they can't think of anything else to talk about. How much your baby sleeps, what time she goes to sleep, how many naps she takes, for how long, etc., etc., etc. And your answers basically determine whether you will be deemed a successful parent or a total failure.

"My baby keeps me up all night."

"Really? Mine has slept through the night since Day One!"

Listen to me, parents of the world. If your child has been sleeping from seven p.m. to seven a.m. from the night you brought him or her back from the hospital, keep your good fortune to yourself. Do not tell the exhausted mother sitting next to you in the park who has clearly not slept in months. WHAT PURPOSE DOES THAT SERVE?

And please, for the love god, DO NOT BRAG ABOUT NAP TIME.

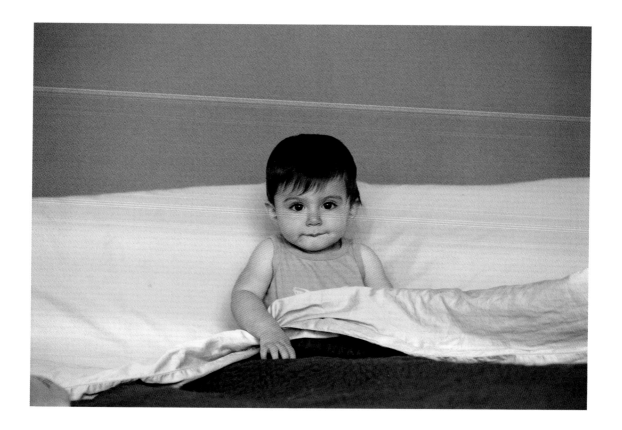

The Most Precious Time Of All: Nap Time

Newborns sleep several times a day. One-year-olds usually nap twice a day, and then by the time your baby hits two, she usually naps once. At three, it's anybody's game. Some kids stop napping entirely. Other kids need the rest and their parents find a way to fit it in.

Phasing out naps is one of the sadder parts of your baby growing up, because if you are at home with your kids, nap time is one of the only times you are free to get stuff done.

Of course, a lot of the time, we have big nap-time plans but then end up getting trapped beneath our sleeping children.

Or you might have the full intention of working, cleaning the house, eating lunch, taking a much-needed shower, etc., but do something stupid instead, like check Facebook, which leads to reading a blog post, which takes you to buy something on Amazon, and then before you know it, the baby starts crying and you've accomplished absolutely nothing.

Timing naps is important. Some parents live and die by their nap-time schedule. You know who they are because they are the same people who always say "No" when you ask them to make plans.

"Sorry, that's Evangeline's nap time. I'd say let's get together earlier but that's Samuel's nap time. Maybe we can get together when they both go to college."

There are other parents who prefer to go about their day and just let their kids fall asleep wherever they may be—whether that's in the carrier, in the stroller, or in the car.

Some parents consider this a huge success.

While others do everything in their power to keep their kids awake so they can have proper naps when they get home.

Some parents might think their kids are done with naps only to have their kids conk out at a totally inconvenient time.

For instance, Harlow fell asleep on the way to her third birthday party. I woke her up because what kid would want to miss her own birthday party? She spent the entire party cranky and crying. I think we all would have had a lot more fun if we had just let her nap through it.

HOW I SPEND THE BABY'S NAP TIME

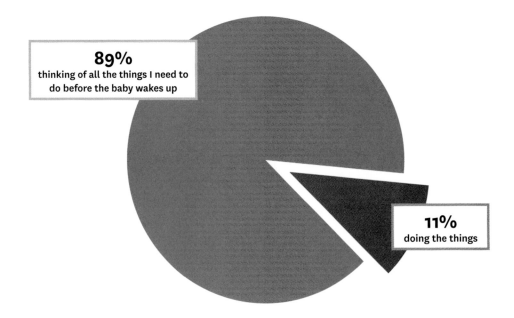

89%
thinking of all the things I need to do before the baby wakes up

11%
doing the things

WHEN SHE'S NOT ONLY AWAKE

SHE'S TAUNTING YOU.

WHEN YOU'VE GOT A BIG DAY OF ERRANDS PLANNED

AND IT'S OVER BEFORE IT STARTED.

WHEN YOU WERE PLANNING ON GETTING SO MUCH DONE

ONCE THE BABY WENT DOWN FOR A NAP

WHEN YOU FINALLY ARRIVE AT YOUR DESTINATION.

Bedtime

As babies, my daughters were both terrible sleepers. They preferred to be awake, hanging out with the grown-ups. They seemed to instinctually know that Mom and Dad were on the couch eating ice cream and watching television, while we expected them to stare at the ceiling in the dark.

I'm a night owl with a major case of FOMO, so nobody understands wanting to stay up late more than I do. But everything you read says that bad bedtime patterns as a baby can mess with your child's temperament for life. Talk about a lot of pressure!

With Mazzy, our nighttime routine would start innocently enough. We'd change her into pajamas, read a book, sing a lullaby, and then, around the second verse, she'd realize what was coming, arch her back like a gymnast, flail her arms, and start SCREAMING. The only way to get her to relax was to force-feed her a

pacifier until she stopped resisting. But even if I somehow managed to get her to nod off, she would immediately jolt awake in a panic, as if I had tricked her and was about to steal all her toys. I ended up spending hours with her in the rocker, trying desperately to get her to sleep in my arms. Then I'd spend another hour making sure she was fully conked out before risking the transfer to her crib. I can't tell you how many times she woke up screaming and I had to start all over again.

I dreaded bedtime. It was stressful for her and stressful for me. So when Mazzy was about seven months old, I started researching sleep training. I studied the Ferber method, the Weissbluth method, and the Sleep Lady Shuffle, testing bits and pieces of their strategies before chickening out.

At the end of the day, the thing that finally worked for us was going cold turkey. I stepped out of the room, shut the door, and did not go back.

I know, I'm a monster. But after just three days, I was a monster with a baby who finally started going to bed at bedtime, sleeping through the night, getting her recommended hours, and waking up with a well-rested smile on her face.

This is why I don't care what the anti–sleep trainers say. It worked for us. It kept us sane and taught Mazzy how to fall asleep.

My mom is anti–sleep training. She was there on the third night of sleep training and when I walked out of the room while Mazzy was still crying, she looked at me like I was breaking her grandchild.

"I never let YOU cry it out," she said.

"Yep, that's right. And I have had trouble sleeping my whole life."

Bedtime Stalling (In 30 Steps)

Mazzy and Harlow may have both been successfully sleep-trained as babies, but as they became toddlers, they each became incredibly advanced in the art of "bedtime stalling." This is the process of prolonging the bedtime routine by any means possible.

It goes a little something like this . . .

STEP 1: Make it as hard as possible for your parents to change you into your pajamas. This can be accomplished by running around the house at full speed and stopping for no one.

STEP 2: Hide.

STEP 3: When they finally catch you, scream, "NOOOOOOOOOOO!!!!!!!" and kick your body out in every direction.

STEP 4: CLING TO THE FLOOR.

STEP 5: Go limp and make yourself as heavy to pick up as possible.

STEP 6: Break free and run into the kitchen, screaming that you're hungry. This works best if you barely ate dinner and your parents fear you will wake up starving at three a.m.

STEP 7: If your parents refuse to open the fridge, ask for a banana. Only the cruelest parent can turn down a toddler's bedtime banana request.

STEP 8: Refer back to "rules for eating a banana" in the previous chapter.

STEP 9: When you have finished eating, don't tell anyone. Wait until they discover you have finished.

STEP 10: Brush your teeth. Spit in the sink. Resume brushing. Keep repeating until someone tells you to hurry up.

STEP 11: Become fascinated with running water and wash your hands for as long as possible.

STEP 12: Become fascinated with towels and dry your hands for as long as possible.

STEP 13: When your parents aren't looking, hide your blankie. Then say you can't go to bed without it.

STEP 14: Take a long time selecting your bedtime book. When you finally select your book, make sure it is the longest one on the shelf. DON'T LET YOUR PARENT TRICK YOU BY SKIPPING PAGES.

STEP 15: When your parent is finished reading your book, beg them to read it again.

STEP 16: When your parent is finished reading the book again, ask for another book.

STEP 17: Suddenly claim a need to pee in the potty, even if (especially if) you have never successfully used the potty before.

STEP 18: Sit on the potty doing absolutely nothing until someone tells you it's time to get up.

STEP 19: After you have been tucked in, complain about something really vague. Example: "It hurts! That thing!" Grunt and squirm for effect while your parent attempts to "fix it."

STEP 20: If you see your parent backing away slowly out the door, you have one option only. "WAAAAAAAAATER!!!!!!"

STEP 21: "NOT THAT CUP, THE OTHER CUP!!!!!"

STEP 22: Ask for a Band-Aid. Actual boo-boo is unnecessary.

STEP 23: Once your parent returns with a Band-Aid, tell them you need a different Band-Aid. For instance, if your parent brings you a *Jake and the Never Land Pirates* Band-Aid, say you want a *Frozen* Band-Aid.

STEP 24: Once you have taken the Band-Aid situation as far as you can, ask your parent to sit in the room with you.

STEP 25: If your parent folds, HAHAHAHAHA-HAHAHAHA!!!! Milk these moments for as long as possible.

STEP 26: If you are still not ready to accept the inevitable, reach down inside yourself, dig as deep as you can, and DO SOMETHING AMAZING. Speak in full sentences, sing the alphabet, count to twenty—anything your parents have been trying and failing to film throughout the day can work.

STEP 27: Once you have run out of material, give a heartfelt "I love you." It's very hard for parents to walk out the door when they are finally getting the adoration they feel they deserve.

STEP 28: At this point, your parent probably feels it is safe to walk out. It's time to start crying.

STEP 29: You have one last card up your sleeve. "KISS AND HUUUUUUUG!!!!!"

STEP 30: Hold on for as long and as tightly as possible.

The Big-Girl Bed Kicked My Ass

When Mazzy was in her crib, the roles were clear. Once we finally got her in bed, she couldn't get out, so she had no choice but to lie there and go to sleep. She never once attempted to climb out. It was a wonderfully magical thing that actually fooled me into thinking that Mazzy was a GOOD SLEEPER.

Nope. Not the case. I have now come to understand that Mazzy was just trapped and defeated.

We switched Mazzy to a "big-girl bed" shortly before her third birthday, while I was pregnant with Harlow. It was not something we wanted to do, but I was told we had to transition her before the baby arrived or else she would harbor negative feelings against her little sister for stealing her stuff.

Since I didn't want to worry about Mazzy smothering her soon-to-be roommate while she slept, we bought a toddler bed, told Mazzy she was a big girl now, and crossed our fingers.

The first couple of nights went swimmingly. Mazzy went to sleep just like she normally did and did not seem to notice the unlimited freedom that her new bed provided.

Then, on the third night—**EVERYTHING WENT TO SHIT.** And by this I mean, any illusions of control we previously thought we held over our toddler disappeared completely.

At about 9:30 p.m., as Mike and I watched a movie on the couch, a tiny figure suddenly appeared before us.

"I'm not tired."

Oh, fuuuuuuuuuck.

> **Mazzy would stay awake for a good two hours in bed before she finally dozed off from sheer exhaustion.**

"It's late, Mazzy. You have to go to sleep."

"Come lie with me, Mommy."

I'd never done that before, as lying down next to your child is not possible when they are in a crib. I must admit, it sounded kind of nice.

Unfortunately, as soon as I laid my head down and bent my legs to fit inside the tiny bed frame, I realized I had made an error in judgment. Mazzy did not want me to sleep next to her. Mazzy wanted entertainment. Stories, songs, conversation, etc. If I attempted to leave, Mazzy would just jump out of bed and follow me out of the room.

For the next few months, we serviced our new bedtime princess with anything her little heart desired. Anything to keep her from getting out of her big-girl bed. We agreed to keep the hall light on, we gave her an endless supply of books to "read" in the dark, and we didn't get mad when we found her hoarding toys under her covers. Mazzy would stay awake for a good two hours in bed before she finally dozed off from sheer exhaustion.

It actually wasn't until Harlow arrived that Mazzy realized she had to be quiet and go to sleep at bedtime, since they shared a room.

Thank you, Harlow.

But then Harlow turned two and we gave her a big-girl bed and everything went to shit all over again.

If you learn one thing from this book, it should be: **KEEP YOUR KID IN THEIR CRIB FOR AS LONG AS POSSIBLE.**

The Family Bed

Childless people think families sleep all together as a personal preference. But that is not always the case.

After we moved Mazzy to her toddler bed, she didn't just have trouble staying in bed at bedtime, she jumped right out when she woke up in the middle of the night, too. I became terrified that at any moment she would suddenly appear at my bedside like the Ghost of Christmas Past, asking me to tell her a story, get her some water, sing her a song, make her a sandwich, find her a day job, explain the theory of relativity, or any other of the many requests she came up with to engage me at three a.m.

I realized it was much easier to pull her into the bed to snuggle than to try to get her to go back to sleep in her own room. One way, everyone gets to continue sleeping and the other usually resulted in tears with the potential to keep you both awake all night.

I'd always put Mazzy in between Mike and me so she couldn't fall out of the bed, and then every night, without fail, Mazzy would slowly turn her body perpendicular to the two of us. Mike maintained his territory, since he sleeps like a rock, but I would find myself balancing on the edge until I was kicked out entirely. And that's just one of many sleep problems only parents understand.

WHEN YOUR KID LIKES TO SLEEP WITH HIS FOOT ON YOUR FACE

WHEN YOUR TINY BABY SOMEHOW FILLS AN ENTIRE MATTRESS

WHEN YOUR TODDLER IS NOT ONLY IN YOUR BED, SHE'S AWAKE!

WHEN YOU HAVE TO BALANCE AT THE EDGE OF THE BED

CHAPTER 9

Are We Having Fun Yet?

Playing sounds fun, right? Your kid is smiling and raring to go. You're like, *Yes, I will give you my undivided attention! We will roll around on the floor, stack blocks, put together a puzzle, and have the kind of mother-daughter moment people become parents for!*

But then you realize the puzzle is two pieces and your daughter wants you to put it together over and over and over again, and suddenly your eyes are closing and your daughter's little voice is getting farther and farther away.

But be careful! Because these are the moments when your child will crawl over to your iPhone and drool on it until it dies. And then you'll wake up, freak out, hightail it to the Apple Store (tyke in tow), and lie through your teeth about how your phone came to encounter water damage. Drool is not covered by your warranty, you know.

TOYS MY TODDLER WANTS TO PLAY WITH

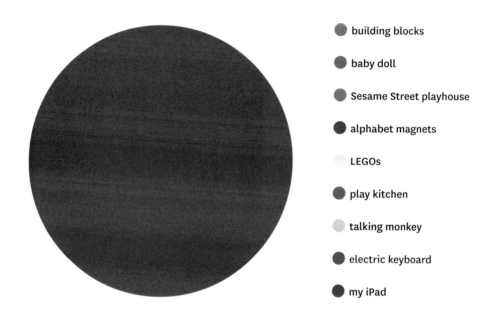

- ● building blocks
- ● baby doll
- ● Sesame Street playhouse
- ● alphabet magnets
- ○ LEGOs
- ● play kitchen
- ○ talking monkey
- ● electric keyboard
- ● my iPad

Yep, there are things you are taught and things you are born with, and wanting to get your hands on the latest Apple products is part of a baby's DNA.

When faced with a room full of age-appropriate toys, what does your kid want to play with? Whatever has a touch screen. You know what Mazzy told me when I told her the iPad was off-limits?

"You have to share."

She wasn't even two at the time.

I let Mazzy use the iPad and she was a pro by eighteen months. Apparently, iPads are so user-friendly, you don't even need a fully formed brain to download Candy Crush. It's not bad parenting, it's raising tech-savvy children.

Which baby do you think is going to come up with the next Facebook? The baby stacking organic unpainted wooden blocks? Or the baby who can intentionally navigate her way to Barbie in Portuguese on YouTube?

Sure, my iPad might be covered with fingerprints and maple syrup, but none of that is going to matter when I'm sixty and living on my own private island that my daughter bought for me after her tech startup went public.

Baby Games

Babies don't need fancy blocks or puzzles to entertain themselves. They can have fun with just about anything. Here are five games your baby plays that you have no chance of winning.

GAME #1: THROW THINGS ON THE FLOOR

How to play: Purposefully drop an item on the ground, pitching a fit as soon as it hits the floor. When your mom picks the item up and hands it back, drop it again. Keep repeating the sequence until your mom looks like she has lost the will to live. If she picks it up again regardless, YOU WIN!

GAME #2: FREE THE TISSUES

How to play: When a box of tissues is left within your reach, dig in and pull out as many as possible. Usually, your mom's first move will be to put all the tissues back into the box—even though they now look like a crumpled mess. Then wait for your mom to become distracted and pull out all the tissues all over again. At this point, your mom will usually stuff the tissues back in the box and move it out of your reach. No matter, you've already won!

GAME #3: SCREECH OR SHRIEK

How to play: Begin the game by shrieking at the refrigerator. This will let your mom know you are ready to play. When she pulls food items out of the fridge, screech to express your dissatisfaction, which will signal to her to choose something else. Alternate between screeches and shrieks with each item presented, until she gives up and hands you a cookie. YOU WIN!

My baby invented a new game. It's called Throw Things on the Floor. I lose every time.

GAME #4: CRUMPLE IMPORTANT PAPERS

How to play: To begin this game, locate your mom's work bag. Remove any and all papers. Then quickly destroy them when your mom isn't paying attention by crumpling, ripping, eating, and dripping the contents of your sippy cup on top of them. Once destroyed papers are discovered, chances are your mom will be pretty angry. But she can't really be mad at you. You are a baby. Therefore, YOU WIN!

I know when Mike thought about having kids he imagined playing ball in the yard, but that's just not how life worked out for him.

GAME #5: CAPTURE THE OLDER SIBLING'S TOY

How to play: Wait until your older sibling has either a) perfectly placed every piece of furniture in her doll house, b) lined up all her Matchbox cars at an imaginary start line, or c) spent hours building a complex city using a variety of different block sets. THEN POUNCE. Grab as many items as you can and hold on like your life depends on it. If your sibling starts screaming and your mom comes running, YOU WIN!

Pretend Play

When my girls reached the toddler years, they became huge fans of dress-up, or as preschools like to call it—pretend play. They pile hats and sunglasses and necklaces on, throw on princess dresses and plastic heels, and prance around the house like fancy little tyrants demanding juice and snacks. They set up elaborate tea parties and demand that Mike and I participate.

I know when Mike thought about having kids he imagined playing ball in the yard, but that's just not how life worked out for him.

The 7 Stages Of A *Frozen* Obsession

Mazzy saw *Frozen* when she was four years old and it was her first experience with a Disney princess movie. She didn't just like *Frozen*. She fell in love with *Frozen*. It became a life-encompassing entity that consumed not just her, but our entire household and everybody in it.

STAGE 1 Your child sees the *Frozen* poster around town and sees the trailer on TV. She calls it the movie with "the funny snowman" and asks to see it.

STAGE 2 You take your child to see the movie. She learns it is not a movie about a funny snowman at all. It is a movie about life, love, betrayal, death, magic, royalty, fashion, troll people, and most important, the two most beautiful sisters who ever lived.

STAGE 3 While playing on the iPad, she stumbles on *Frozen* videos on YouTube. She starts to watch them repeatedly. One day you come home from work and she suddenly knows all the words to "Do You Want to Build a Snowman?" and "Let It Go." In the morning, she asks you to make a braid down the back of her head like Elsa. When you're finished, she gets mad and says, "NO! IT'S SUPPOSED TO COME DOWN OVER ONE SHOULDER!" You pull the braid over to one side but "IT'S NOT GOOD ENOUGH!" You end up starting over and making a diagonal braid from top left to bottom right. She is satisfied. THANK GOD.

STAGE 4 She claims Anna is now her favorite *Frozen* sister. She asks you to call her "Anna" instead of her real name and gets mad every time you forget. She comes home from preschool talking about a fight she had with her friend over who was Anna and who was Elsa. "I'M ANNA, RIGHT, MOM???" "Yes, dear."

STAGE 5 After lots of begging, you buy her Elsa and Anna dolls and a set of *Frozen* miniature figurines. She proceeds to set up the entire city of Arendelle in your living room. Her *Sesame Street*, Hello Kitty, and Olivia figurines all become plebeians in Elsa and Anna's kingdom. She arranges them with more care than you have ever put into anything. After she misbehaves one night, you take away the figurines as punishment. Your daughter reacts like you just abandoned her in a parking lot and she must eat garbage for survival.

<table>
<tr><td>STAGE 6</td></tr>
</table>

STAGE 6 Elsa's doll hair now looks like a rat's nest that might have insects living inside of it. Your daughter insists you take the hair out of the braid and redo it. You then spend the next five hours brushing the knots out of Elsa's hair while your daughter cries that Elsa is bald. You curse Disney for thinking that no child would remove the braid to reveal Elsa doesn't actually have a full head of hair. After six attempts, you finally braid the hair back to your daughter's satisfaction with all bald spots covered. Your daughter now has the words to "For the First Time in Forever" memorized. Only, it's not just the regular "First Time in Forever," it's also the reprise that happens in the ice castle, which is half-spoken dialogue, and she says every word of every character verbatim, like it's just part of the song. She makes you tell *Frozen*-themed stories every night before bed. When you try to get creative and veer off the story line, she tells you that you're doing it wrong and makes you stick to the script.

STAGE 7 Your husband brings home an illegal copy of *Frozen* that he got from someone at his office. Your daughter reacts like you bought her a pony. She ceases to watch anything but *Frozen*. She starts taking her *Frozen* figurines everywhere. To bed, to playdates, to school. You listen to nothing but *Frozen* Radio in the car. She has decided that she will be both Anna and Elsa at all times. Everyone else is allowed to be Kristoff, Sven, or Olaf. At a lunch meeting in Times Square, you are told the Disney Store has just restocked their Anna and Elsa costumes after being sold out

for weeks and you run there like you are in a blind haze, not realizing what you are doing until after you've opened your wallet and are spat back out on the street. You start humming "Love Is an Open Door" with over $100 of *Frozen* costumes in a bag that your daughter didn't even ask you for.

You have bought into it. Your daughter's obsession has become your own.

You are *Frozen*. *Frozen* is you. Don't fight it.

LET IT GO.

Kids Are Sore Losers

Mazzy has now gotten to the age where we can play a few easy card games and board games. This means she has to deal with winning and losing, and while she is pretty good at winning, she SUCKS at losing.

WHEN YOU WANT HIM TO WIN AS BADLY AS HE DOES

BUT HE KEEPS GETTING "DRAW 4 CARDS."

I remember the first time that we played Old Maid, she got upset in the middle of the game because she picked the Old Maid card. I told her it was okay, because the game wasn't over and all she needed was someone else to pick it. Then she pulled her Old Maid card up so it was sticking high above all her other cards and asked Mike to pick one. We laughed because it was a horribly obvious strategy, but at that moment, I knew she was a player, which I can respect.

Although, being competitive and hating to lose are two very different things. I used to think adults lost games on purpose to give their children confidence. Now I know, it's because they don't want to deal with a sore loser.

This is complicated though when your kids are so bad at a game that you must choose between letting them lose and playing it forever.

This is why we don't play Chutes and Ladders anymore. Do you know how many chutes are up near the winning square? It's like the makers were trying to torture parents by making it impossible to win. Two hours in, the kids are crying and the adults are bored out of their goddamn minds. Someone at Hasbro is up there in their executive offices laughing at all of us.

Kids Suck At Hide-And-Seek

Mazzy is almost six. You'd think her game would have improved from a few years ago, when she would forget her feet were attached to her body, and therefore a dead giveaway.

This is particularly funny when she's behind the shower curtain.

At least she's slightly better than her two-year-old sister, who thinks the act of curling up in a ball on the floor is enough to render herself invisible.

Apparently, this is a widespread affliction that affects kids worldwide.

Little kids think just because they can't see us, we can't see them. And if they are standing very still, with their eyes closed and their arms firmly planted at their sides, it's almost impossible to find them. Therefore, finding a semi-decent hiding spot is totally unnecessary.

THE WORST HIDING SPOTS OF ALL TIME

BEHIND A BROOM

BEHIND HIS OWN HANDS

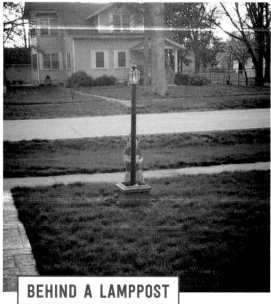

BEHIND A LAMPPOST

NEXT TO THE FRIDGE

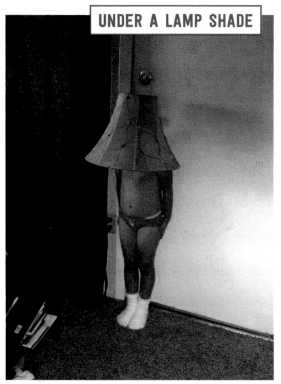

UNDER A LAMP SHADE

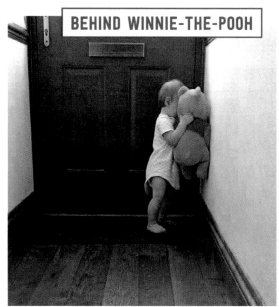

BEHIND WINNIE-THE-POOH

UNDER THE RUG

IN THE HAMPER

10 GAMES YOU CAN PLAY THAT ALLOW YOU TO SNEAK IN A NAP

If all this playing sounds exhausting, I agree. I asked my blog readers to give me suggestions for creative games that don't require consciousness.

1 "We play Road Map, which means I lie on the floor and take a nap as my kids run cars and trucks all over me." —*Elizabeth P.*

2 "I announce that we are playing Pile Things on Mommy, and then lie very still while they pile things on top of me." —*Lindsay S.*

3 "We play *Lion King*. I'm Mufasa, which means I get to play dead while Simba tries and fails to wake me up." —*Kelly H.*

4 "We play hospital. I'm a patient along with all my daughter's stuffed animals. Then I get to snooze while the doctor does her rounds." —*Menai N.*

5 "I lie facedown on the floor and have the girls play 'salon' with my hair." —*Gianna D.*

6 "I say, 'Let's go play on Mommy's bed!' Then Mommy curls up and closes her eyes while toddler jumps, plays, and rearranges pillows and such." —*Kristen M.*

7 "We play Dead Fish. I say, '1, 2, 3 DEAD FISH!!!' and then everybody has to drop to the ground and be very still. First one to move loses." —*Dyan*

8 "There's a 20 minute rule that states you must stay on the floor after being Ninja Turtle nun-chucked to 'death' before you can revive." —*Anita R*

9 "I tell my son that his brother is better at giving back rubs than him. Then I close my eyes and enjoy the competition." —*Emily K*

10 "Frozen is the best game for pretend play. If I'm Anna and my daughter is Elsa, she hits me with her ice powers and then I pass out indefinitely. If I'm Elsa and she's Anna, then I go into my room, shut the door and refuse to play with her. Just like in the story." —*Pam S.*

CHAPTER 10

Crawling, Walking, And Climbing The Walls

Mobility is exciting and should be celebrated! But it also makes your job a lot harder. Most moms (myself included) will brag if their baby does things like roll over and stand up way before their little baby peers. What you don't realize (until you have a five-month-old who's crawling over to outlets and chasing dust bunnies around your house so she can eat them for lunch) is that you want your baby to stay still for as long as possible.

Let me put it this way: What's easier? A baby who you can sit on a blanket, knowing he has no choice but to play with the toys two inches from his body? Or a baby who's trying to climb to the top shelf of your china cabinet to play with the good crystal? (I don't really have any good crystal, but you get my point.)

You want to see your husband freak out? Get your baby to stump him with the remote settings.

I tried to get Mazzy to roll over for the first time like it was my full-time job. I took her through the motions, demonstrated, gave her incentives, and squealed with encouragement. Finally she did it. And then I worked on getting her to crawl by putting her on her stomach and bending her little legs and showing her how she could use them to propel herself across the floor. She started crawling pretty quickly. I was so proud.

But then I realized I had to babyproof everything. And that I couldn't leave her alone in a room to change my socks. And that she liked to crawl over to our cable box and press all the buttons until everything was dubbed over in Japanese.

You want to see your husband freak out? Get your baby to stump him with the remote settings. Oh, the defeat in Mike's eyes when he had to call the cable company to help him fix it.

The best moment was the time I took her to Poppy and Nonna's house (my dad and stepmom) for the weekend.

Let's just say, having a newly mobile baby in a split-level house decorated by people in their sixties who love to shop at yard sales is not relaxing in the least.

Grandpa's Baby Death Trap

We'd been out to my dad's house a few times since Mazzy was born, but this particular weekend was the first time since she started crawling.

We got to the house late on a Friday night, so Mazzy went straight to bed. She woke up at five a.m. and I couldn't get her to go back to sleep. So I decided to take her into the living room to play. As I looked around for a nice spot to lay out some of Mazzy's toys, I was confronted with the hard reality of the situation: **WE WERE SPENDING THE WEEKEND INSIDE A HOUSE OF BABY HORRORS WAITING TO DESCEND UPON OUR CHILD.**

Let's start with the most obvious. The coffee table. A large natural slab of wood complete with horrifically pointy edges and a splinter-inducing finish.

Not to mention that it was sitting on top of a rug that might as well have been a large piece of sandpaper.

What else was in Grandpa's baby death trap?

A FINGER GUILLOTINE (NOTICE HOW A LITTLE HAND CAN EASILY BE PLACED AT THE BASE OF THIS ANTIQUE ROCKING CHAIR)

A TERRIFYING DRAGON (THIS DRAGON IS FIVE FEET TALL)

AN EXPOSED FIREPLACE (DON'T WORRY! A POINTY-EARED METAL CAT IS WATCHING OVER THE LIGHTER!)

AN UNBALANCED WROUGHT IRON SCULPTURE (I CALL IT "THE PHANTOM OF THE OPERA PROJECTILE VOMITED")

A SLEEPING GRANDPA

A SHAKY PEDESTAL (WITH A 20LB SCULPTURE SITTING ON TOP OF IT)

Making the weekend even better was the fact that the one time I left my dad alone with my daughter, he fell asleep. What did Mazzy do? She went straight for the cable box, obviously.

I bet my dad had a lot of fun watching his shows in Japanese.

Pantaloons Of Irony

Leading up to Mazzy's first birthday, my mother-in-law did a very nice thing. She bought Mazzy a dress to wear to her first-birthday party. She presented this dress to me in BIG REVEAL FASHION, which is holding up a closed garment bag and then dramatically pulling back the plastic to reveal the dress on the hanger underneath.

I am not good at letting people down easy, so I prefer to do the opposite. Buy the book, date the guy, give to Greenpeace, fawn over the dress. Even though the dress was not exactly my cup of tea.

It was not a horrible dress. In fact, it was totally appropriate for the occasion. That is, if before the birthday party, our baby would be making a quick detour to accept an Academy Award.

FROM THE QUEEN.

It was also appropriate attire if I'd entered my baby in the Little Miss East Coast Pageantry circuit and her last shot at taking home the crown was to kill it in the Evening Wear category.

Okay, so it looks good in photos, but let me give you the party dress rundown:

★ The top of the dress was black velvet with cap sleeves, which is fancy but fine.

★ The bottom ballooned out into something so gold and sparkly that I feared only leprechauns and the Real Housewives of New Jersey could truly appreciate it.

★ There was a fake diamond brooch in the middle of the bow around the waist. I am pretty sure it had a tracking device alerting Elizabeth Taylor's estate that it was missing from her jewelry box.

★ Underneath the skirt, there was a layer of crinoline. "Crinoline" is a word so absent from my life that I had to do a Google search in order to figure out how to spell it.

★ Under the crinoline, there was a matching pair of GOLD SILK PANTALOONS.

I should mention that Mazzy's first-birthday party was not on a Saturday night, it was on a Sunday at noon. It was not a five-course meal with assorted dancing interludes, it was a rather low-key pancake brunch. And it was not taking place at the White House, it was taking place at my apartment.

Well, turned out the joke was on me, because not only did the dress look amazing on Mazzy, it helped her to walk for the very first time.

How does a dress help a baby to walk? Let me explain.

We'd been trying to get Mazzy to walk for a while, since she started crawling so early. But I think she was so good at crawling that she didn't feel the need to exert the extra effort to stand up. She could quickly get wherever she wanted to go on her knees, thank you very much.

BUT. It turns out, if you put a baby in a dress with a lining of itchy crinoline underneath, crawling becomes a lot more difficult.

She tried her best to crawl, but the crinoline kept getting in her way, plus I don't think she liked how it felt rubbing against her knees. SO. She stood herself up and took her very first steps!

Overachieving Parenting Lesson of the Day:
If you want your baby to start walking, put them in a hoop skirt or an overstarched tuxedo. Lack of mobility will give them the motivation to explore other options.

WHEN YOU REALIZE YOUR KITCHEN CABINETS ARE BASICALLY A LADDER.

WHEN YOU FINALLY FIGURE OUT WHY THE KITCHEN DRAWER KEEPS BREAKING.

And Then They Start Climbing The Walls

Be forewarned, pretty quickly after walking comes running, and then that's when things REALLY get hard, because once your toddler can run, they don't ever want to sit still.

I thought going to a movie would do the trick, and Mazzy started running up and down the aisle. We ended up leaving before the opening credits.

I took her to a bowling party and had to leave because she thought each lane was her own personal runway.

Going to the supermarket where she can run down an aisle, turn the corner, and just vanish? My heart would skip a beat every time she got out of my sight. I didn't understand parents putting their kids on leashes until Mazzy started running.

Some kids would never think of leaving their parents' side or going out of their line of vision, but Mazzy was not one of those kids.

By the time Harlow came along, I knew I wanted to keep her immobile as long as possible, but unfortunately Harlow was Superbaby, and that plan fell by the wayside.

Not only was Harlow crawling by six months, she was pulling herself up to standing, pulling herself up to sitting (which, oddly, came after the standing thing), and clapping for herself, just to drive the whole Superbaby thing home. As if to say, "What? You didn't see my impressive Superbaby feat? Allow me to puncuate it with my own applause."

Harlow didn't just use furniture to pull to standing. She used people. If she climbed up on me while I was on the ground playing with her, that was fine, but if I bent over to pick up a toy and she quickly mounted my back like a poodle in a dog park, we had problems.

I'll never forget the time I turned my head for two seconds, looked back, and she was just sitting on the top of the glass coffee table.

Before Harlow turned two, she wasn't just running, she was whizzing around on a scooter, learning dance moves, jumping from the top of the couch, and probably practicing flying after we all went to bed.

Trust me: You don't want a baby who goes mobile early. Unless you want to lock her in a padded room with Harlow one day.

> If she climbed up on me while I was on the ground playing with her, that was fine, but if I bent over to pick up a toy and she quickly mounted my back like a poodle in a dog park, we had problems.

WHEN YOU REALIZE YOU GAVE BIRTH TO SPIDERGIRL.

WHEN LIFE AS YOU KNOW IT IS OVER.

CHAPTER 11

She Speaks!

Communication is the key to everything and it starts the second your baby exits the womb. "Hi! I'm here! Let me make my presence super clear with an ear-piercing cry!"

They say each cry sounds different and if you pay attention you can decipher which cry means what. There's even a crying analyzer that tells you whether your baby is stressed, annoyed, bored, sleepy, or hungry. I think that's total crap because, in my experience, there are not five reasons a baby cries, there are about 864. Like the cry that says she wants you to pick her up without touching her. Or the cry that means she has developed an overnight aversion to her left shoe.

And what am I supposed to do if my baby is "stressed"? Tell her to work it out in a kickboxing class? What about "annoyed"? Tell my mother to stop calling her? I don't think these options are nearly specific enough.

What part of "WAAAAAHH" don't you understand???

20 Reasons My Baby Cries

1. Oh My God! A stranger is holding me! A stranger is holding me! A stranger is holding me! What's that you say? It's my own father? Oh. My bad.

2. I'm hungry, but that doesn't mean you can just stick a boob in my face. Especially when I've grown accustomed to those amazingly taut bottle nipples while you're at work!

3. Tummy time really blows.

4. Stop putting me in this cradling position. I know that means you are trying to get me to fall asleep.

5. What the fuck is this mashed veggie bullshit??? I SEE YOU EATING BACON ON A BISCUIT OVER THERE!!!

6. Uh-oh. I've stood up and I can't lie down!

7. She's leaving the room. She's leaving the room. She's leaving the room. GASP. She left. SHE'S NEVER COMING BAAAAAAAAAAAACCCK!!!!!!!!!! Oh. She's back. Phew.

8. That girl who calls herself my sister keeps stealing my toys and claiming they were HERS before I got here. WTF? Like there was life before I got here?! Pfffffft.

9. Why do you insist on removing the carpet lint every time I successfully get it into my mouth??? All my hard work for NOTHING!

10. NO! Not the tub draining sound! That's TERRIFYING!

11. I HATE THE CAR SEAT!

12. You know what's worse than the car seat? Being in the car seat and then THE CAR STOPPING. Is it a red light? Traffic? Road construction? I CAN'T HANDLE BEING IN A CAR AND NOT MOVING AT THE SAME TIME!!!

13. Hear that sound? That's the sound of my pacifier falling through the crib slats AGAIN.

14. This is what you get for taking me to a restaurant with only a small plastic bag full of Puffs that I finished in .02 seconds.

15. Don't you GET IT??? Life is so much better when YOU'RE HOLDING ME!!!!

16. Oh no. You're not going to like this, but—IT'S. UP. THE. BACK.

17. NOT THE SUNSCREEN AGAIN!!!!! Didn't I just put that on yesterday???

18. What is that horrible noise??? Turn it off! Turn it off!! Turn it off!!! Is that adult music?? Well, adult music sucks! It's got no farm animal sounds whatsoever!

19. You put my blankie IN THE WASH??? Now that's just CRUEL.

20. NOOOOOOOO!!!!! YOU'RE DOING SOMETHING FOR YOURSEEEEEELLLLFFFF!!!!!!!!!!

The First Word

Your baby's first word is incredibly exciting. It might be "Mom," it might be "Dad," it might be "ball," or you might be raising some supergenius whose first word is "neuroscience." Who knows? Every baby is different.

Mazzy's first word was "hi" at five months and she said it to every passing stranger on the street, which makes total sense because she has since grown up to be the most social kid alive. Honestly, I think saying "hi" so early and seeing the reaction she got when she said it to other people really shaped a lot of her personality.

The key to a first word really being a first word and not just something that mistakenly fell out of your baby's mouth is the ability to use it in the correct context.

In public, Mazzy stuck to the use of "hi" as a traditional greeting, but at home she found more creative uses. For instance, if your attention was focused elsewhere (like on your laptop), she would crawl up your leg and yell, "Hi! Hi! Hi!" to get the focus back on her. She'd also say "hi" in a gruff tone when you came to fetch her out of

her crib in the morning, as if to say, "You should have been here sooner." And most disturbing, she'd look me in the eye and say it in the middle of breast-feeding, like she wanted small talk over dinner.

Mazzy's second word was "Boo." "Boo" is what she calls her blankie, which she still has, by the way. It's short for "peekaboo," which we played using the blankie all the time. Clever, right? But her third word was her favorite and the word she used the most often. Her third word was none other than "Da-Da."

Saying "Da-Da" before "Ma-Ma" is supposedly par for the course. Every parenting book says that babies have an easier time pronouncing the "da" sound than the "ma" sound. As a result, babies usually say "Da-Da" first, having nothing to do with whom they are addressing.

Well, that might be true for OTHER BABIES, but it was pretty clear Mazzy knew exactly to whom she was referring.

When she woke up in the morning (even though I was usually Responder #1), the first words out of her mouth were—"Da-Da!" No, she was not calling me "Da-Da" by mistake. Her tone was not "Nice to see you." It was more like "Take me to your leader!" Plus, she accompanied her demand with a finger pointed straight for our bedroom. As soon as she caught the first glimpse of my husband (still in bed), her tone switched from demanding to triumphant. "Da-Da!!!"

Mazzy then informed me (in so many words) that she would not have the bandwidth to focus on "Ma-Ma" until she had perfected "Da-Da" into the more proper form of "Da-dee." And then, once she got it down, she began her favorite new pastime—saying it in quick succession. Mike would pour a bowl of cereal—"Da-dee! Da-dee!" He'd sort the mail. "Da-dee! Da-dee! Da-dee!" He'd put his coat in the closet. "Da-dee! Da-dee! Da-dee! Da-dee!" Like he was her favorite sports team and his completion of mundane household tasks relied on her extreme fan dedication.

"Ma-Ma" had to be her next word, right?

Wrong.

Next came "ba-ba" (bottle) and "nah-nah-nah" (banana).

Soon after, "uh-oh," "no-no," and "yum" all became part of her repertoire. Followed by "ball," "book," "bye-bye," and (don't judge me) "iPad."

"iPad" was particularly disheartening.

She began saying the word "apple" so perfectly that I wondered if she was getting diction coaching while everybody else was sleeping.

And there I was, repeating "Ma-Ma" like a broken record. So hopeful that one day she would honor me with the courtesy of addressing me by name.

At twelve months, Mazzy started stringing words together. She'd say "Hi, bay-bee" when she saw herself in the mirror. "I love you" was "I la la." Don't even get me started on "Hi, Da-dee!" and "Bye-bye, Da-dee!" It was heartbreaking!

Finally, at thirteen months, when Mike and I were away on our first vacation, Mazzy said "Ma-Ma" when she saw me over Skype. Maybe she never felt the need to say it because I was always there?

I said, "Thanks, honey. It's about fucking time."

Time To Stop Cursing

At first, Mazzy was just saying words that we were actively teaching her. But then she started busting out tougher words like "tissue," "doctor," and "knapsack." This is the moment when we realized we had to stop any sort of swearing whatsoever.

FUCK.

I remember one fine morning, I closed our front door and immediately realized I had locked my keys inside.

"OH SHIT!" I yelled without thinking.

You can bet Mazzy repeated "Oh shit!" for the rest of the day.

Kids copy everything grown-ups say, and nothing sounds more interesting to repeat than a spontaneous word shouted at top volume.

If you've spent a lifetime swearing, it can be tough to curb your habits. Obviously, a well-placed "motherfucker" is always more effective than a half-assed "fiddlesticks," but I can think of many word combinations that technically don't include profanities but sound just as insulting—like twitwaffle or dumpster clown.

Actually, I'd probably lock Mazzy in her room for calling someone a dumpster clown.

Parenting is hard. Cursing is an art form. Tread lightly, my friends . . .

Early Talkers And The Snuffleupagus Syndrome

Nowadays, everybody on *Sesame Street* is fully aware of Snuffleupagus. But back when I was a kid, everybody thought he was Big Bird's imaginary friend. I wanted so badly for the rest of the gang to know Big Bird wasn't making Snuffy up. And it was always so close! Snuffleupagus would have to go home to brush his teeth or something and then two seconds later Maria and Gordon would show up and be all like, "Big Bird is such a liar!" It was EXCRUCIATING.

This is how I felt when I would try to show off Mazzy's advanced vocabulary to my friends. She'd be talking up a storm, acting like a GENIUS BABY, when she and I were alone, and then in front of friends, Mazzy would clam up and act all REGULAR BABY. And then everybody would be nodding, like *Mm-hmm, just another crazy mom who thinks her kid is soooooooooo freakin' special.*

At the time, I felt the need to show off that she was super smart. Why? I don't know. Maybe

because I never got to brag about having a good sleeper.

But now I know that early talking doesn't necessarily mean early admittance to Harvard. Everybody catches up. And there will be things all the other kids are doing way earlier than your kid that you don't want rubbed in your face.

Like potty training. But that's a story for another chapter.

So enjoy your baby's newfound genius. But keep quiet. Brag to Grandma if you must. She's really the only one who cares.

Late Talkers Can Communicate, Too

Harlow was much slower to start talking. She preferred to use a series of head shakes and shrieks to communicate. Also, just to prove that siblings can be very different, the only word that Harlow ever used was "Ma-Ma."

She'd scream "Ma-Ma" until she was blue in the face.

"Ma-Ma. Ma-Ma. Ma-Ma. Ma-Ma. MA-MA!!!!!!!!!!!!!!!!!"

There was probably an additional "Ma-Ma," but it was so loud and high-pitched that only dogs could hear it.

Made me wistful for the Mazzy "Da-Da" phase, that's for sure.

Especially since Harlow used "Ma-ma" to refer to everyone—Daddy, Mazzy, Grammy . . . pretty much anyone with the ability to pick her up off her precious feet so that they never had to touch the ground. GOD FORBID.

Harlow might not have had the language skills that Mazzy had at the same age, but she was just as opinionated and could communicate just as clearly. She didn't just shake her head "no," she shook her whole body in adamant defiance. And if I'm honest, Harlow's shrieks were way more effective than asking for something with words.

Harlow's shrieks convinced us to let her keep the pacifier, even though the doctor told us to get rid of it.

Harlow's shrieks convinced us to put off transitioning from a bottle to a cup.

Harlow's shrieks convinced us to let her wander around the apartment chomping on a bagel instead of forcing her to eat at the table like everybody else.

Hmmmm. Maybe Harlow is the one who's getting early admittance to Harvard.

Toddler-Speak Translated

As your kids get older and go beyond words to phrases, full sentences, and conversations, that's when things get really fun.

Although, be careful, because sometimes what kids say and what they mean are a little off the mark. And by "off the mark" I mean "sneaky and manipulative."

If you pay attention, there's a lot more you can glean from a simple "No, thank you" than you think. For instance, in certain contexts "No, thank you" means "I look forward to continually rejecting green vegetables until I'm eighteen and move out of the house."

WHAT MY TODDLER SAYS

WHAT MY TODDLER MEANS

WHAT MY TODDLER SAYS	WHAT MY TODDLER MEANS
"AGAIN!"	"Spin me around 40 times or until you throw your back out. Whichever comes first."
"Can I share with you?"	"I am going to take your toy."
"I don't have to poop."	"I have to poop."
"Yummy . . . delicious chicken."	"How many pieces do I have to eat before I get a cookie?"
"Can we buy ice cream?"	"If you don't buy me ice cream, I will start screaming so loudly, passersby will begin to suspect abuse."
"I want DADDY!"	"Daddy will buy me some ice cream."
"I love you, Mommy."	"It's bedtime and I am trying to charm you into letting me stay up late."
"I want to call Grandma."	"I want to look at pictures on the phone while Grandma talks to herself."
"YAY! THE POOL!!!!"	"Get one step closer with that sunscreen and I will cut you."
"Are we there yet?"	"If you thought the torture on Route 24 was bad, you just wait until you spend four hours trapped in a car with a two-year-old."
"You look pretty."	"I'm going to find your lipstick and write with it on my bedding."
"I want to sit on the counter."	"I know that's where you keep the iPad."

Totally Butchered Words

Even if you do stop cursing and shield your kids' ears from swearwords outside the home, your kids will probably still end up saying a few unfortunate things anyway. This is because toddlers might be trying to say one thing, but then it comes out sounding like another word entirely.

This wouldn't be a big deal if that other word was something super cute. Like, if your daughter mispronounces "bathing suit" to sound like "baby soup," but the problem comes when the mispronunciation makes your two-year-old sound like a trucker.

Here are more words totally butchered by toddlers. It's important to note—these are actual mispronunciations submitted by their parents. I am not making this stuff up. Even I don't swear this badly.

MANCAKES

TITTIES

COOTER

DUMB FUCK

GIRL CHEESE

BITCH

PENIS BUTTER

You can't really continue
a chapter after you've
thrown out the word
"penis butter," so I think
I will just meet you in
chapter 12. Don't forget
the cockporn!

Pooping And The Potty

Let's start with changing diapers, which literally takes up three-quarters of your day when you have a newborn. For the first time in your life, pooping will be something you actually discuss out loud. Not only will you discuss it, you might even text your spouse pictures of poop with captions like "Does this look normal?" or "Check out the size of the grown-man log that came out of our baby girl!!!!"

You'll probably want to delete those pictures before you accidentally upload them to Facebook. Or flip through them on your phone while showing off photos of your new baby to coworkers in a client meeting.

This chapter will discuss all things potty, like your new preschool-level vocabulary. For instance, you probably haven't said the word "poop" since you were five years old and here you are having lengthy conversations about it with your spouse.

Remember that guy/girl who pledged their undying love to you over champagne and passed canapés? Yeah. Parenthood just changed the ending to that fairy tale completely.

The Diaper Blowout: A Parenting Rite Of Passage

Allow me to paint the scene.

It was early evening. Mazzy was about four months old. She was fed and getting our full attention, but acting moody and distracted regardless.

Then she made the face. You know the face? Confusion mixed with extreme concentration.

It stunk immediately.

Mike and I looked at each other, instinctually knowing this was going to be a two-person job.

Before we even made it to the changing table, we discovered the poop had traveled straight up her back. We detoured to the bathroom.

Mike held Mazzy dangling over the tub while I stripped off her clothes.

I reached the diaper. It was COVERED. Inside and out.

I looked at Mike. Surely he would impart *some knowledge* on a method for hands-free poop removal. The man has a preferred method for EVERYTHING—from the best way to cut an avocado to the proper way to refill a hand-soap canister.

Uh . . . Mike?

Mike shrugged. He had nothing.

I took a deep breath and carefully unfastened one diaper tab. Then the other. Then I summoned up all my surgical expertise and attempted to remove the diaper with as little movement as possib—

Mazzy kicked her leg.

It splattered.

Not just anywhere.

ON MY FACE.

Mike laughed and laughed in a way that said, "This image of you with shit splatter on your face will be ingrained forever."

For better, for worse, indeed.

How Not To Change A Diaper

When Mazzy was born, we repurposed a dresser as a changing table and put one of those foam contoured changing pads on top.

There were two straps on the bottom of the pad that looked like they were meant to attach the pad to the dresser, but since I had come up with the ingenious idea of putting a rubber mat underneath so that the pad wouldn't slip, I cut those stupid straps off.

In the very beginning, changing Mazzy's diaper was more of a bonding moment than a chore. She'd stare up at me while making tiny little movements with her hands and legs as I gently explained what we were doing. (New moms think every moment is an educational opportunity.)

"First I am going to unsnap your onesie . . . then I am going to remove your diaper. . . ."

Once I got the hang of it, I felt almost proud of my increasing agility with those little flip tabs.

I was a diaper-changing natural!

Flash forward six months.

Not only had Mazzy developed an extreme hatred of being changed, she had also developed ridiculous back muscles, so that when I picked up her feet, she'd arch her back in the air and spin herself toward the wall so that literally only the top of her head was still touching the table.

I would stand there dumbfounded with my daughter's butt in my face as her body writhed about and I did my best to keep a firm grasp on her legs. Otherwise, she would surely catapult herself across the room, taking all the poop with her.

How could anyone possibly get a diaper on a baby this acrobatic?

"You know what someone should invent?" I brought up to Mike after a particularly harrowing changing experience. "A diaper pad that has straps to hold the baby in place."

"You mean like the diaper straps you cut off?"

"What? Oh . . . right."

That's what those straps were for.

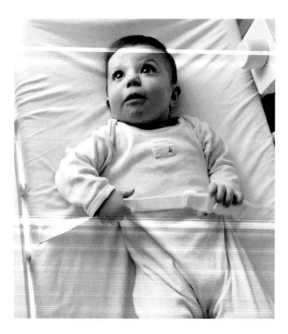

Potty Training

At some point after Mazzy turned two, I bought her a potty. I had no big plans to train her just yet, but I was told I should get her familiarized with the process.

Mazzy was not interested in actually using the potty but she did seem to understand that it had a certain power over me. For instance, if I said she had to go to bed, pretending she was ready to use the potty was an excellent stalling tactic.

When Mazzy was around two and a half, I decided the potty was not a reading station or a procrastination device, but a place in which my daughter should actually pee and poop. I think it was the day she crossed her arms, stomped her foot, and said . . .

"I want to wear diapers FOREVER!!!!"

The next weekend, with the fear that my daughter would INDEED be the kid who goes to college still in diapers, I forgot everything I ever said about waiting for her to tell me she was ready and forced the issue.

I put up a chart. I bought a bag of M&M's. I let her choose a "grand prize" for when she had successfully peed in the potty twelve times. Lastly, I told her that she would not be training alone. We would be training her stuffed Minnie Mouse, too.

For the record, she was not on board with any of this until Minnie Mouse entered the picture.

Obviously, I'm no expert. I parent with bribes and stuffed rodents. And we were not even a little bit successful. But I learned a lot. Here's your opportunity to learn from my mistakes . . .

10 Things I Wish Someone Had Told Me About Potty Training

1. Just because you have a seemingly intelligent child doesn't mean they can follow simple instructions like—how to wipe from front to back. I realized my daughter didn't even know the difference between her "tushie" and her "pagina."

2. Making fun of parents who would dare to use something as ridiculous as the iPotty prior to actually training a child yourself will suddenly seem very silly once your child has convinced you to let them use the iPad on the potty.

3. Every instinct you have ever had about piss and shit will disappear. You will cheer. You will describe. You will admire. You will triumphantly walk that bowl of crap over to the toilet all together like it's THE SHIT PARADE and this is the world's greatest family bonding moment.

4. If you think your child has mastered potty training within half a day, that is the exact moment they will forget everything they've learned and pee inside a car seat sitting on the floor in your hallway.

5. If you are in the middle of potty training and your child decides to randomly sit inside their car seat, be suspicious. Be very, very suspicious.

6. If your child's favorite pooping corner is also where she keeps a stockpile of favorite blankies and stuffed animals, you might want to put those items away and line that spot with plastic like Dexter's kill room.

7. Remembering to use the potty while fully naked is an entirely different skill than remembering to use the potty while wearing pants and underwear. Think algebra as compared to calculus.

8. Peeing in the potty is a totally different skill than pooping in the potty. Think earth science as compared to physics.

9. For every M&M your child eats, be prepared to eat ten yourself.

10. When you reach the end of your potty training chart and you're cheering, "YAY! My daughter is potty trained!!!" she might start crying because she thought at the end of it she'd get to go back to wearing diapers.

OH NO,
SHE DIDN'T

A Shitty Story

One night, Mike was feeding Harlow a bottle in the nursery while I was reading on the couch to Mazzy.

Suddenly, he called my name in a very alarmed fashion.

"Ilana! Get in here!"

I dropped the book, left Mazzy on the couch, and went to see what was the matter.

"What is it?"

Mike remained in the glider feeding Harlow while he pointed to the corner of the room looking absolutely horrified.

"WHAT. IS. THAT???"

I looked.

gasp

A huge ugly turd was sitting on the floor next to Mazzy's pink patent-leather shoes. We'd been having issues with Mazzy refusing to poop in the potty, but this was uncharted territory.

I kept my distance. "Is that what I think it is?"

"I don't know. YOU are the one closest to it. You tell me," my husband said, still seated.

Mind you, this was probably the only time in the history of the baby that Mike was the one feeding Harlow before bedtime. And then there I was, responsible for inspecting and probably cleaning

Mazzy took a few steps closer to inspect. "Don't touch it!" I yelled as visions of poop-stained hands streaking our wallpaper filled my head.

up what was clearly a shitastically solid mound of preschooler poop.

"Mazzy!" I called.

Mazzy came in.

"What, Mom?"

"Did you poop in the corner?"

"No."

"Mazzy . . ."

"I didn't poop."

"It's okay, honey. We all make mistakes. You just have to tell us. How long has it been there?"

"I didn't poop, Mom."

Mazzy took a few steps closer to inspect. "Don't touch it!" I yelled as visions of poop-stained hands streaking our wallpaper filled my head. I left to get a paper towel and came back with the whole roll. It wasn't until I had the wad of paper towels cupping the turd that I realized something.

Mazzy was right. She didn't poop. Nobody did.

She had just outed my twenty-year-old Monchichi for sporting a toupee.

ARE YOU READY TO START POTTY TRAINING?

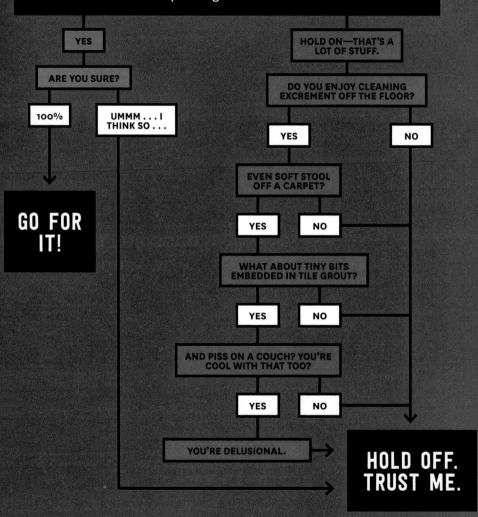

Does your child dislike being in wet or soiled diapers, tell you when he needs to go to the potty, know how to pull his pants up and down by himself, understand the inner mechanics of a toilet and approach the concept with great enthusiasm?

YES

ARE YOU SURE?

100%

UMMM . . . I THINK SO . . .

GO FOR IT!

HOLD ON—THAT'S A LOT OF STUFF.

DO YOU ENJOY CLEANING EXCREMENT OFF THE FLOOR?

YES　　**NO**

EVEN SOFT STOOL OFF A CARPET?

YES　　**NO**

WHAT ABOUT TINY BITS EMBEDDED IN TILE GROUT?

YES　　**NO**

AND PISS ON A COUCH? YOU'RE COOL WITH THAT TOO?

YES　　**NO**

YOU'RE DELUSIONAL.

HOLD OFF. TRUST ME.

The Benefit Of Waiting

My experience has taught me that the longer you wait to potty train, the easier the process. Sure, you won't get bragging rights among your friends when your one-year-old very politely asks to use "the loo," but you will have way fewer accidents and much less mess.

There are few times in your life you can opt to take the easy route and come out on top, and potty training is one of them. TAKE ADVANTAGE.

Both my girls fell on the later side of the spectrum. Harlow wouldn't even go near a potty until she turned three.

Here's the thing. All those parents who tell you their kids were potty trained at eighteen months, they're probably lugging portable potties to the playground and running into random restaurants on a regular basis with potty emergencies.

That's not potty trained. Real potty training happens when your kids have enough bladder control to hold it in until they can make it to the bathroom themselves. It's not pooping in a potty in your living room.

When Mazzy was 3.3 years old, she collected her potty training prize. Initially, she had asked for a LEGO castle, but then changed her mind and asked for something else.

"I want a pink furry caterpillar."

"A what?"

"A pink furry caterpillar."

Rather than ask why, I said, "Okay. I'll see what I can do."

Luckily, the Internet exists and a parent can google "pink furry caterpillar plush toy" to see what comes up. You know what I found?

THIS:

You know what I didn't do?
Check the measurements on the damn thing.

Congrats on potty training, Mazzy. May you outgrow your ginormous caterpillar as quickly as possible.

3

LIVING THE MOM LIFE

CHAPTER 13

Where Did My House Go?

It's ironic that you spend so much time nesting to prepare for when the baby arrives, because once that baby gets there, your house, your home, your sanctuary, whatever you want to call it—it isn't yours anymore. It belongs to them.

Let's take a trip down memory lane to when I decorated my nursery. Actually, let's rewind even further, back before I had a baby, when I considered home décor pretty important. At some point in my twenties, I cared less about clothes and more about what my apartment looked like. I agonized over throw pillow choices, spent over a year selecting our bedroom curtains, and stopped using my favorite shampoo because they changed the packaging to something that looked ugly in our shower. Beyond my clothes and some books, I didn't really have much in the way of stuff. I moved often in my twenties and found packing a good opportunity to declutter.

Did I really need the vase an ex had given me as a housewarming gift five years ago? No, I didn't. Was I ever going to create the shelving system I had imagined when I started my snow globe collection as a kid? No, I wasn't. Did I see myself wearing cowboy boots again? Not even a little.

"The amount of thought I put into designing Mazzy's nursery is borderline embarrassing.

changed his mind. Then I opened the door to the spare bedroom and there was Mike, lying on his bed, watching television in exactly the same setup as his old apartment. Basically, he had taken all his things and re-created his room in my apartment.

"Where did you sleep last night, Mike?"

"In here," he answered meekly.

From that point through when we got married until we had our first child, the second bedroom was his room. We slept together in the master bedroom of course, but all his clothes, his books, his shoes, etc., were in the spare bedroom. Like he had a really big closet.

When we had Mazzy, I didn't want a half nursery/half man cave, so for the first time, Mike and I really blended our things, made sacrifices, and found room for both of us in the master bedroom. But to this day, you will still find Mike's ties hanging on the back of the closet door in the nursery.

The amount of thought I put into designing Mazzy's nursery is borderline embarrassing. This was in pre-Pinterest times, which I know seems crazy. (In addition to sourcing home décor ideas in magazines, we were carting ourselves around the city in horse-drawn buggies!)

With every move, I streamlined my belongings to the bare essentials. My apartment was easy to keep neat because there was not much to put away. Plus, I had a full extra bedroom to store whatever I didn't want in the main living space. For most of my single life in my apartment, I rented that extra bedroom to a roommate, who moved out about a year before Mike moved in.

On the weekend Mike moved in, I happened to be away for work. I thought I was going to come home to a complete disaster area but was surprised when I walked in the door to find that nothing had changed. I walked from the living room to the bedroom and everything was exactly as I had left it. I briefly wondered if Mike had

In lieu of a Pinterest board, I created a mood board in Adobe InDesign with pictures of each item I was planning on purchasing, including furniture, bedding, and artwork. I worked on that mood board for months, swapping out different gliders and mobiles until I had the most perfect room possible.

When the room was painted and fully furnished, it was my favorite room in our apartment. What could possibly destroy the oasis I had lovingly created in our now overcrowded two-bedroom apartment?

How about putting an ACTUAL BABY in it?

By the time our baby started to move, only a couple months after her arrival, she armed herself with an agenda that I call: Project Nursery Takedown (PNT).

PNT began when Mazzy first learned to stand. The bookshelf had to be rearranged for safety purposes.

For the safety of the child or for the safety of the items, I am not sure.

The next strike involved a large mirror hanging over the changing table. Mazzy started kicking it. Harder and with more of an intent to destroy each time. To retaliate, we decided we'd better anchor it to the wall, and I contacted a handyman to do it. There was some issue with the studs in the wall and I came home to a golf ball–sized hole where the mirror used to be.

The next blow came when the weather turned cold and we started wearing jeans. What can jeans do to harm a nursery? Well, when jeans are worn on a cream-color cotton twill glider chair, the dye can rub off into the fabric and create a big blue mess. Kinda like the Cat in the Hat just paid you a visit. You can wash the fabric but then it will just happen all over again, so I decided to throw a white sheet over the whole thing, like a dead body waiting for burial.

The last straw was when the beautiful hand-made mobile (not handmade by me; I had found it on Etsy) had the misfortune of falling on Mazzy while she slept. Mazzy was fine, but by the time I arrived on the scene, she had crumpled and chewed that mobile like it was breakfast.

Project Nursery Takedown was complete.

Worst Roommates Ever

It is impossible to live with order and cleanliness when you live with children. Beyond the nursery

The Jumperoo alone can take up your whole house.

destruction, there are many ways the addition of a child can ruin your home, so let's break it down into two parts.

PART 1: CLUTTER

Mess involves two things—the fact that there is a ridiculous amount of stuff in your apartment and the fact that you do not have adequate space to put it away. Or your kids don't willingly put it away. Or they think they are putting it away, but putting it away to them means lining everything up in a very specific order across your dining room floor and then telling anybody that comes near not to touch it.

Have you lived with a tower of blocks on your coffee table that you were forbidden to take down even though you could only see the top of Stephen Colbert's head when you watched *The Late Show* from the couch?

Currently, I am sitting at my kitchen counter on my laptop. Right behind me is a scooter/stroller

parking lot blocking my way to the washer and dryer. Next to my couch is a kid-sized table and chairs that has no business being there. Behind the dining room table there is a mini toy kitchen shoved into the only available wall space. On top of the credenza is about one thousand assorted accessories for princess and Barbie dolls. On top of the dining room table is a pumpkin decorated with feathers, a woodshop project (that looks like Mazzy nailed random pieces of wood scraps together), and a fruit bowl not just full of fruit but also full of potty training stickers, crayons, and those dollar-store goodie bag items you get at birthday parties that your kids won't let you throw out.

This is not a playroom—this is my living and dining room. I live in Manhattan. To afford an apartment with a playroom, I would have to be Beyoncé.

Before Mazzy was born, I reupholstered an ottoman to put in the living room. It was supposed to house all the toys. Isn't that hilarious? It fits maybe 5 percent of them, and if you put something in there, you might as well dump it in the trash because you aren't going to open that thing again for the next five years.

Every spot in my apartment has been overtaken by my kids' stuff. Their plastic plates and cups spill out of our cabinets, their books consume our nightstands, their stuffed animals take up permanent residence in our bed, etc., etc.

Once upon a time, their bedroom (aka Mike's room) was the place we put all the stuff we didn't want seen in the rest of our apartment. Since they arrived, we have no junk room and ten times as much junk.

How Does This Stuff Accumulate?

PRESENTS: From your baby shower and every birthday beyond, people think the only way to show they care is with a gift. I actually appreciate the people who show up empty-handed. We don't have enough room for the toys as it is. And if you think birthdays are bad, the holidays are even worse. It's not only about showing your kids you care about them, it's solidifying their belief in Santa. Or in my case, making sure Hanukkah seems just as fun as Christmas.

BIRTHDAY GOODIE BAGS: Why do goodie bags exist? You've already shown the kids a good time and given them cake, do they really need to leave with a parting bag, too? There are two options for goodie bags—candy or cheap presents. I used to appreciate the dollar-store gifts more than the candy because I didn't want to give my kids unhealthy snacks, but now I think—at least with a pack of M&M's—they can eat it and throw away the wrapper.

ART PROJECTS: It starts in preschool. Your daughter comes home with a painting she made in class. You hang it on the fridge and say it's beautiful, even though it's a small scribble on one corner of a very large piece of paper. The next day, she brings home five more. And the next day five more, until the pile of preschool artwork is so high and so wide, you can't find the surface of your dining room table. You try to throw some out but she catches you and you fear this means she's going to lose all faith in her budding aritistic abilities. You vow never to throw out her artwork again. Or at least get better about doing it when she isn't looking.

GRANDPARENTS: My mother called me from the store the other day with a question that began "I'm trying to find something to give to the girls at Thanksgiving. . . ." I have no idea what she said next because—"I'm sorry, why do the girls need Thanksgiving presents?" My advice to you is: Don't try to reason with a grandparent trying to spoil her grandchild. She's got a master plan at work.

As your kid grows, the stuff changes but it does not go away. There are numerous LEGOs that must be accounted for, Barbie shoes to organize, princess dress-up clothes that must remain accessible, in addition to all the stuff that you actually NEED for your children.

Sometimes I look around our apartment and am momentarily confused because I think I have mistakenly stumbled into the stockroom of a Babies"R"Us.

Before I got pregnant, I had dreams of buying a new couch but knew it was a silly thing to do right before I started having kids. Now I treat our old couch like it's my last soldier standing in the baby war zone. No matter how many toys surround it, I always make sure its pillows are perfectly fluffed, the throw is folded just so, and the back is squared perfectly with the wall. It's a minor victory, but at the moment it's the only one I've got.

GRAMMY'S MASTER PLAN

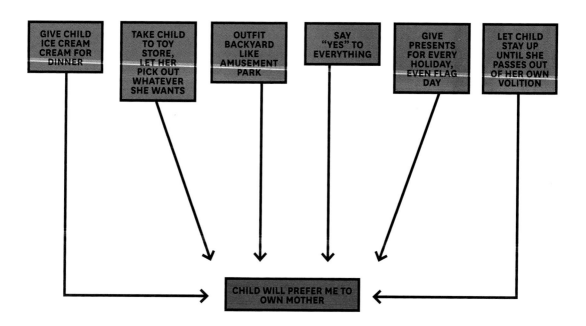

SCENES FROM A TODDLER'S HOUSE

WHEN YOU'RE NOT ALLOWED UP THE STAIRS.

WHEN YOU ORGANIZED THE TOY BIN TWO SECONDS AGO.

WHEN YOUR DINING ROOM TABLE IS CONVERTED INTO A PARKING LOT.

WHEN YOUR HOME LOOKS LIKE IT SHOULD BE ON

"HOARDERS: PRESCHOOL ARTWORK EDITION."

WHEN YOUR SIPPY CUP COLLECTION HAS EXCEEDED THE DRYING SPACE.

WHEN YOU TELL YOUR KID TO PICK OUT A BEDTIME BOOK.

WHEN YOU HAVE TO DECONSTRUCT A FORT

EVERY TIME YOU WANT TO SIT ON THE COUCH.

WHEN YOUR BATHROOM SINK LOOKS LIKE A SCENE FROM THE BACHELOR.

PART 2: CLEANLINESS

Back in my twenties, before I was married with kids, only a certain amount of dust, crumbs, and bathroom grime accumulated in my apartment. I probably stretched out my bathroom cleaner and my jumbo bottle of detergent a full year before I needed to replenish.

Now, with a husband and two little kids at home, I find myself cleaning up spills, wiping down countertops, and spraying our glass coffee table on a daily basis. **What exactly am I cleaning up?**

1) TOOTHPASTE SPIT

When I brush my teeth, I brush for a decent amount of time and then spit directly down the drain. Mazzy, on the other hand, barely brushes and then spits as close to the edge of the sink as possible, creating a big blue blotch a full mile from the drain, where water does not reach. I scrub that blue spot off my sink every single night.

2) SYRUP DRIPPINGS

Harlow is a big fan of waffles. She eats them every morning. Waffles, unfortunately, are always accompanied by syrup. Syrup has a way of migrating off the plate to the table, off the table onto the chair, off the chair onto the floor, and then off the floor onto your shoes, so you track it everywhere in your house.

3) BATHTUB GRIME

You'd think poop would be the grossest thing you'd ever have to clean up, but the tub is a whole other story. Throwing dirty kids, bubbles, and bath wash into one big tub leaves a lovely ring of grayish fuzz that makes you wonder if anybody is even getting clean in there. And if your child poops in the tub? Then you just have to move.

4) PRINCESS DUST

No, I'm not talking about the kind that sparkles and makes magical fairy godmothers appear. I'm talking about the dust that accumulates around various princess knickknacks that seem to multiply on a daily basis. And it's not just the princesses. It's the My Little Ponys, the LEGO Friends, the Little Pet Shop figurines etc., all arranged in careful curation that Mazzy refuses to move. Dusting has never been so complicated.

5) SNOTTY TISSUES

Most people throw dirty tissues directly in the trash. Mazzy and Harlow like their dirty tissues to keep them company on the couch. During a particularly bad cold season, it is not uncommon to lose my children entirely in a pile of their own Kleenex.

6) FINGERPRINT SMUDGES

If my children ever tried to steal something, the cops would find them so fast it would be laughable. That's because they leave fingerprints so defined, you don't need a black light to see them. Their iPads look like a crime scene.

7) PLAY-DOH CRUMBS

If glitter is the herpes of craft supplies, then Play-Doh is syphilis. I'm speaking specifically about those dried little bits that find their way into every nook and cranny of your home. I've been dust-busting the same Play-Doh hair salon incident since 2013.

8) DIRTY SOCKS

Mazzy and Harlow's favorite thing to do is figure skate in their socks. In a way, sock skating is great because it can have the added benefit of picking up unwanted crumbs, Play-Doh, yogurt, syrup, and glitter off the floor. On the other hand, it is one of the many, many, many things my children do that creates a ton of laundry.

WHEN YOU HAVE HUNDREDS OF SOCKS

BUT NOT ONE MATCH.

Never Trust Your Kids When They're Too Quiet

Let's end this chapter with some of the biggest messes ever created by little kids. This is what happens when you go to the bathroom for five seconds or you step out of the room to take a phone call. Messes such as these can happen when you least expect them, so it's best to be on guard at all times. Even if you think your spouse is watching the kids. *Especially* if it's your spouse watching the kids.

When it gets quiet, your kid could be practicing his reading skills. Or your kid might be . . .

POURING OUT EVERY BOX OF CEREAL IN THE PANTRY.

SLATHERING HERSELF IN NUTELLA.

DESTROYING YOUR IPHONE AND TRYING TO SAVE IT WITH RICE.

DIPPING HERSELF INTO A BUCKET OF HOUSE PAINT.

GOING TO TOWN WITH YOUR MASCARA.

RIPPING APART A BEANBAG CHAIR.

BATHING IN GLITTER.

CHAPTER 14

Celebrating The Big Stuff

If you have a child, chances are you've been to your fair share of birthday parties. I thought I had a social life in my twenties but that's NOTHING compared to what Mazzy's got going on at age six. Our social calendar pretty much revolves around where she can get free pizza and cake.

But before the dawn of drop-off parties (which is a truly awesome milestone), there are the baby birthdays, which are way more about the parents than the kids. You kept your baby alive all year! You deserve a piece of cake. Want a super easy birthday party theme? For Harlow's first birthday we had a pancake pajama party. We served pancakes, had a cereal bar, and nobody (not even the adults) had to get dressed!

JACKSON
BEST CAKE BEARD

LILAH
BEST FORK SUBSTITUTE

The 1st Birthday

You did it! It's your baby's first birthday. Now that you've reached the finish line, it's time to give your baby back and go on with your lives!

Just kidding. You'll probably throw a party first.

There are all different kinds of first-birthday parties you can throw—from a small family affair to a full-on gala with two hundred of your baby's closest friends. Just be honest with yourself, the party is to impress *your* friends, not your baby's. SHE HAS NO FRIENDS. She can't even talk.

A word of caution though: I went to a one-year-old's birthday party where the parents went all out with a magician, a balloon guy, a bouncy castle, a chocolate fountain, a D.J., and a bubble machine. That baby hid under the table the entire time.

Any way you slice it, you want to give your one-year-old their very first bite of cake.

Or perhaps you've been feeding your baby Reese's Peanut Butter Cups and Pop Rocks from the very beginning. No judgments!

Yes, judgments. If you can't withhold Kit Kats and Snickers now, how the hell are you going to steal their Halloween candy one day when they aren't looking?

Also, if you don't save their first taste of frosting for their first birthday, you are really missing out on a key photo-taking opportunity. Whether your kid loves cake (and then never

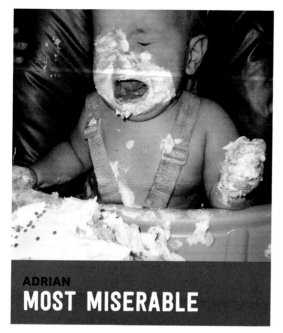

ADRIAN
MOST MISERABLE

ADLEY
BIGGEST SUGAR HIGH

wants to eat a vegetable again) or hates it (THIS MUST NOT BE MY CHILD!!!), this is a memory you won't soon forget.

The Worst Goodie Bags Ever

For both Mazzy and Harlow, we held simple parties at home with family and our closest friends. The only difference is—at Harlow's party all the kids left with a new pair of slippers in their goodie bags (it was a Pancake Pajama Party) and at Mazzy's party, all the kids left with a raging stomach virus. That's what we get for not picking a theme straight from Pinterest. We were so thoughtful (it being our first kid and all), we even gave the virus to some of the adults! Mike and I included, unfortunately.

I don't know if the virus stemmed from Mazzy or another child at the party, but a week later, after we had all finally stopped throwing up and wondering if our legs would ever let us walk again, we found out that almost everyone in attendance had just had an equally horrific week.

Video evidence from the party showed Mazzy eating off of every single person's plate. It was like watching a scene from *Contagion*, showing precisely how the germs were transmitted person to person via a vessel, i.e., my daughter.

Let's just say it was an interesting set of thank-you cards that year.

Dear Uncle Scott,

Thank you for coming to my birthday! I loved the Tickle Me Elmo! I hope you enjoyed the diarrhea you got in return.

Love,
Mazzy

Speaking of thank-you cards, why do parents always write these cards from the perspective of the baby? Do they think they're fooling anyone? Is Uncle Scott reading his card thinking, *Oh, I'm so glad Mazzy really liked my present! I was worried. If I knew she could write, I would have gotten her a pad of paper!*

Yep, thank-you cards are all a big pack of lies. If they were really written by the baby, they'd be a lot more honest.

> "You know what's harder than writing fifty thank-you cards in the voice of your kid? Forcing your six-year-old to sign her name to each one.

Here's a tip: Buy a plain cake and then decorate the shit out of it. This cake was my proudest mom moment and I baked nothing whatsoever.

BRUTALLY HONEST THANK-YOU CARDS

Dear Poppy,

Thank you for the tremendous dollhouse! My dad had the absolute worst time putting it together. I heard him use some colorful language while searching for a missing piece, so it's provided a lesson in new vocabulary, too! My mom is pissed that it's too large to fit in my room and must take up permanent space in the living room. I don't know why she's so attached to the coffee table.

Peace out,
Harlow

Dear Aunt Robyn,

Thank you for the shirt with the stain on it! I'm guessing it's a hand-me-down from my cousin, which is fine. You could have just said that instead of putting it in a box and wrapping it. For future reference, a shirt with a Circo tag in a Baby Gap box is a DEAD GIVEAWAY.

Love,
Harlow

Dear Uncle Eric,

Wow! The baby drum set is really fantastic! I've been trying to figure out something that would drive my mother crazy and now I have it! How did you know????

Love,
Harlow

Dear Grandma Toby,

Thank you for the hand-knitted sweater! The colors are beautiful (although atrocious when you put them all together). Also, the neck hole is sized for a giant. When I tried it on, my mom said I looked like I was in Flashdance. I don't know what that means but I don't think it's good.

Love,
Harlow

Dear Mazzy,

Thank you for the drawing. It looks like it took you a full three minutes to do. I'm happy that even on my birthday you stayed true to yourself and showed me the most minimal attention possible. I also like how you gave yourself a beautiful pink dress with hearts on it, while I am naked. Again. Very true to life.

I love you,
Harlow

Dear Aunt Pam,

Thanks for the beading kit. Even though I won't be able to use it for another five years. Maybe if you came to visit me once in your life you'd realize I am a baby with very limited fine motor skills. You should really check the ages the toy is appropriate for. It says it right on the box!

Love,
Harlow

When Mazzy turned four, it became clear we could no longer contain (nor entertain) a bunch of big kids in our small NYC apartment and started researching birthday party venue options. Dance parties, gymnastics parties, soccer parties, cooking parties, pottery parties, robot-making parties, etc.

We have been to them all.

Most birthday party venues have packages for a set number of guests and then you have to pay per head for additional kids. And even then, there is still a cap. When Mazzy was in preschool, she basically had the same class of friends who would move up year after year. But by the time she was in kindergarten, she'd accumulated a wide variety of friends from all walks of a young person's life (school friends, playground friends, family friends) and we couldn't invite everybody. Especially when every kid comes with a set of parents and possibly a sibling.

Who was the first to go? The same family members who had been there year in and year out. Uncle Scott was kicked out by Mazzy's six-year-old classmate. Same went for Grammy. My sister still holds a grudge about this. (Love you, Sis!)

We ended up having her friend party on the weekend and inviting family over to celebrate on Mazzy's actual birthday. This meant twice as many presents and twice as many thank-you cards.

You know what's harder than writing fifty thank-you cards in the voice of your kid? Forcing your six-year-old to sign her name to each one.

CHAPTER 15

Are You Ready For Baby #2?

Many parents have a kid with the expectation they will have a second one. But this decision should not be made lightly. You have to decide when the timing is right, if this is indeed a good decision, and how your current child will deal with the news. Usually people decide to have a second kid when everything normalizes with the first. They're ~~sleeping a little more~~ regularly, they've stopped crying all the time, you've started wearing pants without elastic waistbands, etc.

Then they think, "Hmmm . . . I'm feeling semi-normal again. Like I'm starting to get everything under control. Wouldn't this be the perfect time to screw all that newfound sanity up?!"

Parents. We're gluttons for punishment.

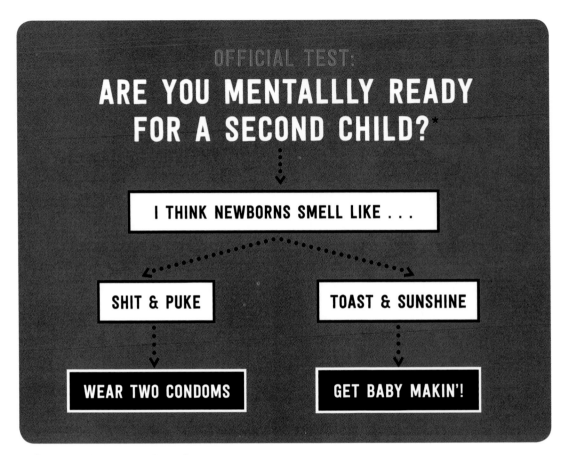

OFFICIAL TEST:

ARE YOU MENTALLLY READY FOR A SECOND CHILD?*

I THINK NEWBORNS SMELL LIKE . . .

SHIT & PUKE → WEAR TWO CONDOMS

TOAST & SUNSHINE → GET BABY MAKIN'!

*This test is 100% foolproof.

If you're a mom, don't worry—adding a second kid to the equation isn't that much different than you probably imagine. If you're a dad, well, wake the hell up, because this new kid is going to rock your world. At least that's what happened with Mike.

My belief is that in most instances, second children affect dads more than moms because moms are usually all in with the first, whereas dads think they're all in, but they're also still escaping to go to the gym every once in a while. Even if they aren't going to the gym, they still know it's out there as an option. I know there are dads out there who are different and honestly, I'm not even coming down on dads for not being all in, I'm just saying once there are two kids, it's one parent per child. That's when the equal partner thing really starts to kick in.

With a second kid, both parents are on duty at all times and it can be a pretty tough adjustment

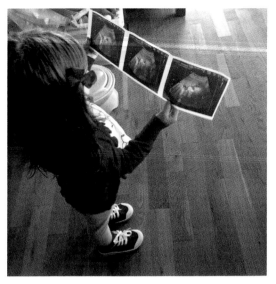

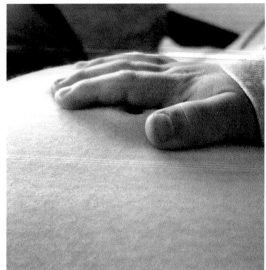

for those who are still using the occasional Saturday for golfing outings (ahem). Two kids eliminates your freedom completely. "Me time" is basically haircuts and late-night runs to the grocery store, which explains why my husband's favorite thing is coming home to discover we are out of milk.

Yep, parenthood will turn buying milk into an eagerly anticipated activity and your mandatory trip to the dentist into a vacation.

My husband is at the store right now. This is what it's come to—a need for bananas so great, it can't wait until morning.

Pregnant With Toddler

Assuming you found the time and stamina to get pregnant, you now have to deal with nausea and your toddler at the same time. Sound like fun? The good news is, you might not be able to put your toddler on your lap anymore, but you will bond with her in a whole new way.

Because pregnant women and toddlers are basically one and the same.

12 Ways A Pregnant Woman Is Just Like A Toddler

1. THEY DEMAND PEOPLE GET THEM THINGS.

Being pregnant is the greatest excuse in the book to make your husband get you things. "I want ice cream." "We don't have ice cream."

"I guess you'll have to go to the store then." Kind of like the way your toddler is screaming for juice right about . . . NOW.

2. THEY ARE PRONE TO DRAMATIC MOOD SWINGS.

Harlow will cry hysterically because she doesn't want to go to the playground and then, all of a sudden, she'll stop, smile, and scream excitedly, "Go playground!!!" Uh, sure, kid—whatever you say. Which is probably the same reaction my husband had to me when I would be on top of the world, catch a glimpse of my large, pregnant self in the mirror, and start sobbing uncontrollably.

3. THEY HAVE WEIRD FOOD OBSESSIONS.

When I was pregnant, I was obsessed with gazpacho. I wanted to eat it for every single meal of the day. If it wasn't for bread, Harlow would be on a yogurt-only diet. She actually likes to drink yogurt smoothies with a side of regular yogurt. She calls it "yogurt and yogurt" and that's all she craves morning, noon, and night. "I want yogurt and yogurt!" "It's five a.m., Harlow." "YOGURT AND YOGURT!!!" All right, fine. Just like there is no arguing with a pregnant woman, there is no arguing with a toddler.

4. THEY GROW AT ALARMING RATES.

In nine months, a pregnant woman can gain twenty-five to fifty pounds, popping buttons on her shirts and rendering pant zippers useless, until she is forced to buy a whole new maternity wardrobe. Toddlers don't fare much better. Pants I bought my daughter just a few months ago are suddenly too short, T-shirts are unintentionally showing her tummy, and her feet have grown two sizes since this past summer.

5. THEY EXPECT PEOPLE TO READ THEIR MINDS.

When I was pregnant, I routinely cried to my husband for no other reason than he should know what was wrong, even if I had no idea myself. This morning, my daughter had a screaming fit about something. I think it had to do with her *Frozen* spoon, judging by the way she was waving it around like a crazy person. Was it dirty? Did she want the Minnie Mouse spoon instead? Would she have preferred a fork? I have no idea. I rarely do.

6. THEY LOSE THEIR MINDS WHEN THEY GET HUNGRY.

When I was pregnant, I kept crackers on hand at all times because if I ever was in situation when I got hungry and didn't have something to eat, I would unleash a holy terror on whoever happened to be standing nearby. I recognize this same holy terror when my toddler gets hungry and I can't find an acceptable snack in my bag. Unfortunately, the terror is unleashed directly at me. Karma is a bitch.

7. THEY LOSE THINGS CONSTANTLY.

While I was pregnant, I was in a constant state of exhaustion. What little brain capacity I had left was dedicated to my day job and memorizing every page of my pregnancy books. If you asked me where my coat or my keys were? I was like a toddler trying to locate her sippy cup. Or her blankie. Or the blue crayon. Or Anna's cape. For the seventeenth time that afternoon.

8. THEY REQUIRE CONSTANT PRAISE AND ENCOURAGEMENT.

The surest way to get toddlers to do something is to praise them. Eat a piece of broccoli? "Well done!" Brush her own hair? "Good job!" Put the square peg in the circle hole? "Nice try!" Pregnant women aren't that much different. They want compliments. "You don't look like you've even gained a pound!" They want thanks. "Thanks for trying to make dinner even though you passed out while the water was boiling!" They want appreciation. "Thank you for carrying my child. That's the only gift you ever have to give me."

9. THEY ARE CONTINUALLY REDECORATING.

If you're pregnant, they call it "nesting." I remember moving the furniture in the nursery endlessly before deciding on the best configuration. Likewise, my toddler has now decided our bedroom duvet belongs on the floor and the pillows on the couch can be put to much better use as beds for her stuffed animals. Tomorrow she'll probably decide her *Sesame Street* playhouse belongs in the bathroom, and her potty belongs in the kitchen. And don't even try to move the pile of building blocks on the coffee table. They might look like a mess to you, but to a toddler, that's "urban planning."

10. THEY WILL NEVER SAY NO TO ICE CREAM.

Although, to be fair, I'm not currently pregnant and I won't pass it up, either.

11. THEY ARE THE MOST INDECISIVE EATERS ON EARTH.

I remember telling my husband I was in the mood for Chinese and by the time it was delivered, I could think of nothing more disgusting. Ditto for every toddler I know. How many times have you been asked to open a string cheese, only to have it rejected when you are done?

12. EVEN WHEN THEY MAKE IT TO THE POTTY, THEY'VE PROBABLY PEED A LITTLE IN THEIR PANTS ON THE WAY.

Why You Should Have Two Kids

If you want a serious reason to have a second child, I present you with **Photo Evidence:**

That's my two girls looking absolutely freaking adorable together. Mazzy was totally enamored with Harlow the second she saw her and has been in love ever since.

In fact, Mazzy brought a lollipop to the hospital to give to her newborn baby sister.

"Mazzy, babies can't eat lollipops. . . . "

"Oh, that's right! I guess I'll eat it myself then."

Harlow doesn't always return Mazzy's affection, but seeing my girls together is probably the single most beautiful thing I've ever witnessed as a parent. It beats sunsets, the ocean, and

Nutella-covered graham crackers, which is pretty amazing if you think about it.

But beyond the beauty of seeing your two children together, second siblings give your first-born something to do. Eventually that newborn becomes a playmate—someone for her to play Barbies with or role-play *Frozen* or toss a ball to so you can sip your cup of coffee slowly on your own. Or your cocktail. Whatever you prefer.

Trust me, it's worth it. Says the mom who somehow found time to write a book.

You'll also learn that taking care of a new baby is way easier than taking care of your toddler. When I had Harlow, it was interesting to think back to when we first brought Mazzy home and try to understand what we thought was so challenging about it.

Newborns eat, poop, and sleep. Mostly, they sleep. Easy-peasy. Most important, newborns are your one-way ticket to staying home in your pj's while delegating toddler care to your spouse, with no guilt whatsoever!

Hmmmm . . . maybe I should have a third.

Is It Friend Or Foe?

There is the possibility that your firstborn will not be so enthusiastic about her new baby brother or sister. If that's the case, please take comfort in the knowledge that you are not alone.

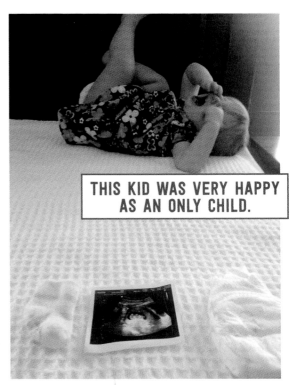

THIS KID WAS VERY HAPPY AS AN ONLY CHILD.

THIS KID WAS ALREADY OUTNUMBERED.

THIS KID LIKED HIS OLD T-SHIRT, THANK YOU VERY MUCH.

THIS KID REALLY WANTED A NEW TRAIN SET.

THIS KID DOESN'T WANT TO LEARN TO DO ANY OF THOSE THINGS.

THIS KID IS PLOTTING REVENGE.

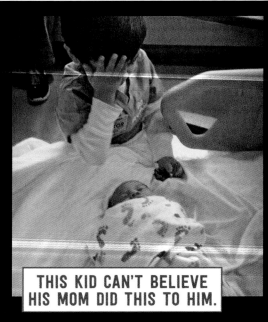

THIS KID CAN'T BELIEVE HIS MOM DID THIS TO HIM.

THIS KID CAN'T BELIEVE HIS MOM DID THIS TO HIM AGAIN.

(YEP, IT'S THE SAME KID ONE YEAR LATER.)

Mastering Your Parenting Style

When you have a child, you hear endlessly about different parenting styles—helicopter, tiger, authoritative, attachment—it can all be a bit overwhelming. Especially since most of the parenting styles I see out in the world today require a lot of stamina.

Have you ever seen those parents who talk to their kids nonstop, like every waking, breathing moment is an opportunity for a lesson? Or what about the parents hovering over their kids at the playground, making sure they never attempt the big slide or the jungle gym? Someone went up to Harlow once to save her from climbing a ladder. That person looked at me like I wasn't doing my job. "It's fine," I said. "Because I've let her climb a ladder, she knows how to climb a ladder."

I went to my sister's for lunch the other day and she was sitting there, feeding her two-year-old with puppets on her hands. ACTUAL PUPPETS. A dog and an owl. I'm sure her puppet show was delightfully entertaining and educational, too. One-woman-show parenting? Is that a style? I don't know, but I bet my nephew giggled throughout *and* ate all his vegetables.

I bought finger puppets once. Back in the beginning, when I still thought I had something to offer in the children's entertainment arena. My lame-ass puppet show bored me to tears within two minutes. I am definitely not a one-woman-show kind of parent.

The good news is that you can easily invent your own parenting style. One that suits you and doesn't make you crazy. If you call it a "style," criticism is a lot easier to swallow. They don't think you're a bad mom. They just disagree with your *parenting style*.

Don't you feel better already?

Here's a simple quiz to determine your parenting style.

Your kid trips while running in the playground. Your first reaction is to:

a. Run over and scoop her into your arms before she even realizes she touched the ground.

b. Panic and call the hospital.

c. Explain the theory of gravity.

d. Yell "Shake it off."

If you picked D, you have a parenting style just like me!

When Mazzy was really little, this wasn't my initial instinct. I was as fearful of my baby getting hurt as the next mom, but Mike was pretty adamant about not coddling her. He'd yell, "Shake it off!" in a casual tone, like a stumble was no big deal. Nine times out of ten, she'd pick herself back up, do a little shake, and keep on going. Once I saw how effective his approach was, I adopted it myself.

Now, if my kid falls, I don't run over to immediately hug the hurt away, screaming, "ARE YOU OKAY?! ARE YOU OKAY!!!!?????" I try not to inform her reaction with my own. If I sound upset, they will be, too. This is a fact. Even if the boo-boo is purely imaginary. I like to wait a beat to see if she is really hurt or upset before I gauge my own reaction.

To the casual observer, it might look like Mike and I are less attentive parents, but we actually have a real strategy in place. If you catch your kids every time they fall, how are they going to learn their limits?

Listen, I'm sure there are numerous advantages to being hovered over—feeling loved and protected, for example. But instead of feeling guilty for things you aren't doing, just remember there are advantages and disadvantages on both sides.

For instance, when you are actively engaging with your kids—making up games, copying crafts from Pinterest, going over flash cards, etc.—that's awesome. But do you know what also breeds creativity? Boredom. Kids need space to play on their own, find their own sense of identity, and express themselves in ways you wouldn't imagine.

Restricting your kid's diet to organic food and keeping a close watch over sugar intake could create healthy habits that last a lifetime. It could

SUPERMOM PREREQUISITE SKILLS

- Feeling satiated from a diet of table scraps and Goldfish crackers
- Making a three-course meal with only one hand
- Wrestling an alligator into pajamas
- Easily eliminating all curse words from the English language
- Always keeping one eye on the china cabinet
- Being able to read *Goodnight Moon* fifty times in a row without throwing yourself out a window
- Catching pacifiers right before they hit the ground
- Smelling poop from across a playground
- Pushing an empty stroller with one hand while carrying a fussy toddler in the other
- Resisting the urge to turn on the television at every waking moment

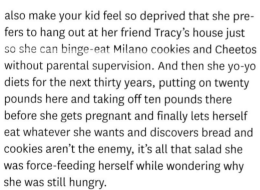

also make your kid feel so deprived that she prefers to hang out at her friend Tracy's house just so she can binge-eat Milano cookies and Cheetos without parental supervision. And then she yo-yo diets for the next thirty years, putting on twenty pounds here and taking off ten pounds there before she gets pregnant and finally lets herself eat whatever she wants and discovers bread and cookies aren't the enemy, it's all that salad she was force-feeding herself while wondering why she was still hungry.

Uhhhh . . . I think I just got lost in therapy there for a moment. Where was I? Ah, yes.

There are positives and negatives to everything and nobody at this early stage of the game knows which way it's going to go.

If you love your kid, provide a safe environment, and model good behavior, you are way ahead of the game. Even if you never make sandwiches in the shapes of elephants or create a catalog of Pinterest-worthy toddler activities for a rainy day.

So don't blame yourself when your kid seeks therapy in twenty years. If you had hovered over them, they would probably be seeking therapy then, too. Just for a different reason.

Nobody is Supermom. And really, do you even want to be?

Lies I Tell My Kids

Here's another reason why I'm not Supermom. I'm a big fat liar. Sometimes it's way easier to get your kids to comply by lying through your teeth than by giving a wishy-washy "No." Less questions and complaints if they think they're asking for something illegal rather than something you just don't want to give them.

For instance, did you know the iPad doesn't work in the car except if we are on really long road trips? And the playground closes right around nap time? Also, we have a box of cookies that depletes itself rather quickly ("Sorry, hon, there are none left") and then refills itself magically overnight.

Which is a good thing, because eating too many sweets can result in a TRIP TO THE HOSPITAL. Much like crossing the street without holding an adult's hand, which is AGAINST THE LAW.

As is wearing pajamas to school.

Speaking of school, did you know they won't let you in if you haven't taken a bath? Yep, they will literally lock the doors and bar your entrance.

There is also a toy store we pass quite regularly that is less a place to buy toys and more of a TOY MUSEUM. Sometimes the $3 animal figurines by the front counter are available for purchase, but the five-story dollhouses, the $100 block sets and the miniature drum kits are for DISPLAY ONLY.

Have you seen the ice cream truck lately? Not the one that sells "pretend ice cream" (we see that one all the time), but the one that legitimately sells real ice cream. That one is much harder to find.

And don't try to play the "Hokey Pokey" on iTunes more than three times in a row, because

Does parenthood immediately inaugurate you into a world of compulsive liars?

the computer will break. Yep, a whole day needs to pass before it is safe to play it again.

Caillou, Curious George, and Strawberry Shortcake all go to bed at the exact same time as my daughter, so if she wakes up in the middle of the night, there is no way to watch them on television.

Does parenthood immediately inaugurate you into a world of compulsive liars?

Don't ask me . . . I'm too busy counting the days until I can reveal my severe allergy to dogs. And cats. All animals, really. Even reptiles.

I've had that gem ready since my mother told it to me.

She still stands by it.

LIAR.

A Liar's Guide To Good Behavior

If you want some more assurance that you're not the only one lying to your kids, here's a whole list of parents who do the same. Obviously, a lot of these only work when your kids are really little, so you should use them to your full advantage while you can.

1. "The ice cream truck only plays music when they are OUT of ice cream." —*Jen*

2. "We have traumatized our son with fake phone calls to the mayor of our town to let him know a child in his district was not eating his vegetables." —*Kristin*

Dear tooth fairy,
This is Sawyer's room. He lost his tooth on Tuesday and you forgot him. Please come back tonight!
Love,
Sawyer (+ his mom)

3. "Spider-Man eats all HIS dinner." —*Synnove*

4. "No one goes outside to play after the sun goes down." —*Synnove*

5. "That animal by the side of the road? Sleeping." —*Angela*

6. "The Chicago Bears are so awesome that even Doc McStuffins and Dora drop everything, including their time slots, to watch them, and therefore there is nothing else on TV." —*Katy*

7. "Chuck E. Cheese is only open for birthday parties." —*Kristin*

8. "I can tell when they're lying, because their eyes change color. This is a double win for me, because my eyes obviously do not change color when I tell them this, which proves I'm not lying!" —*Lindsay*

9. "I have a special pair of glasses that can see if you used your toothbrush." —*Lisa*

10. "It's against the law for five-year-olds to ride in strollers." —*Lanei*

11. "The Tooth Fairy is no good and lazy, which is why she was a no-show." —*Stacey*

The mother of all lies, of course, is Santa, who is really just one big bribe to get your kids to behave all year in return for presents. I might be Jewish, but I know how Christmas operates.

Somehow We Survived Our Parents

If you want proof that your kids will be okay even if you aren't 100 percent focused on them 100 percent of the time, look no further than your own childhood.

Did your mom pack well-balanced, colorful bento boxes for your lunch? Or did she jam a PB&J in a plastic bag? Did your parents come up with creative family activities every weekend? Or did they stick you in front of the TV to watch Saturday-morning cartoons?

The expectations for parenting were far lower when we were kids. The safety standards were almost nonexistent. And most of us turned out just fine.

Here are fifteen things our parents did that would get them arrested if they did them today.

They made their liquor super accessible.

They let us ride bikes without helmets.

They dealt with the pain of pregnancy with a smoke and a stiff drink.

They thought the stove was a perfectly fine place to put the bouncer.

They let us parasail in adult-sized harnesses.

They thought this was a car seat.

They put those car seats in the front seat.

They let us ride in car seats on the back of a motorcycle.

They tried to trap us in playpens that weren't put together correctly.

They let us relax with a beer.

They thought it was hilarious when we smoked cigarettes.

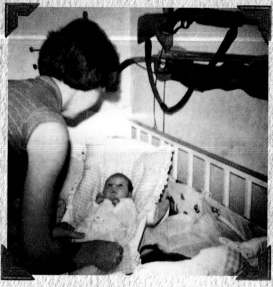

They thought "above the crib" was a great place to hang a gun rack.

They let us hang out in a glass house with a lion.

They thought it was perfectly safe for our older brother to drag us in a cart by a rope.

They took family photos in front of their marijuana plant.

CHAPTER 17

Objects of Affection

At two years old, Mazzy decided a cheap green plastic tractor shaped like a frog was her brother. His name is Henry, and she still speaks of him fondly.

When Mazzy was five, we found that frog tractor while going through some old toys in storage. Mazzy's eyes went soft as she remembered the tractor's significance.

"That's Henry," she said nostalgically.

"Do you remember who Henry is?" I asked.

Mazzy nodded. "MY BROTHER."

~~Harlow~~ carried around a purse for a full year. She wears sunglasses like it's her job. She is ~~currently~~ going through a phase where she must have "her stuff" with her at all times. Her stuff includes a pink dolphin she lovingly refers to as "Dolphinie," a pink blankie, a silver water thermos, and a purple Dora compass, which she calls her "phone." She likes to sleep with her "phone" at night just like I do.

Kids get attached to weird stuff, and often parents go to great lengths to honor the importance of these relationships. You have no idea how many times I have searched high and low for Harlow's "phone" in order to ensure a smooth transition to bedtime. And Mike and I have never come closer to divorce than the time he lost Mazzy's Boo in the mall. He found it, THANK GOD, or else Harlow might never have been born.

Boo is the single most important item in our household, for the past six years and running. More important than water, more important than shelter, and definitely more important than ME.

The Importance Of Boo

Let me tell you a story. More of a saga, really . . . When Mazzy was a wee little thing, still swaddled in a bassinet by my bedside, I read (somewhere online, I bet) that a good way to transition a baby from a bassinet in your room to a crib in their own room is to give them a piece of your clothing to sleep with. This way, they would have your scent with them throughout the night.

With that in mind, I took two old cotton tank tops and sewed them together to make a little blankie. (When I say I sewed them together, I

mean that I took them to the dry cleaner's to see if the tailor could sew them for me. He did it on the spot for free. Thank you, Million Dollar Cleaners!)

Every night, I would place the blankie in the crib next to Mazzy while she slept. Mostly, she ignored it. But I kept it up just in case.

After a month or two, I noticed that she had started sleeping with her head on it like a pillow. If we wanted her to take a nap in the stroller, all we had to do was lay it over her eyes and she was out. If she started crying, I'd hand it to her for instant comfort.

I patted myself on the back for a job well done.

Gradually, Mazzy's attachment grew until one day she suddenly couldn't live without it. She'd point to it as soon as they were separated. She'd crawl somewhere, realize she had left it behind, and then crawl back to retrieve it. If I took her out of the crib while the blankie was still lying inside, all hell broke loose.

Her undying devotion was made even more apparent when she began to refer to it by name. She called it "Boo," due to our use of the blankie when we played peekaboo.

"Boo?" (Where is my Boo?)

"BOO!" (I SEE BOO! GET ME BOO NOW!!!)

"Booooooooo." (Aaaaaaah. I have my Boo.)

I remember one night, Mazzy woke up sick and I took her back to our bed. I lay Boo over my chest as a signal for her to put her head down to rest. We both lay still for a moment, and then abruptly, Mazzy sat up and threw up everywhere. Me, my pajamas, the bed—everything was soaked. Literally, puddles of puke formed around me in the sheets like a log in a river. Mazzy was crying and I (not knowing how to get up without

spreading the devastation) screamed for Mike to wake up and help.

Mike flicked on the light to survey the situation. Sick, crying baby. Puke-drenched wife. River of throw-up running through the bed. Do you know what got my husband's immediate attention?

Boo.

Puke-soaked Boo was whisked away as if it were in the throes of cardiac arrest and the washing machine was the only thing that could revive it. Only after Boo was safely spinning its way back to life did Mike come back to toss me a towel and retrieve the baby.

But I didn't blame him. Without Boo, there was no sleep. There was no ability to take Mazzy away for the weekend. There was no peace in the car. There was no leaving her with strangers. Boo was as important to us as it was to Mazzy.

That night, we spent the next hour all together waiting for Boo to complete both its wash and dry cycles.

Mazzy, exhausted and miserable, repeating, "Boo? Boo? Boo? Boo? Boo? Boo?"

The ending buzzer finally sounded, the dryer door was pulled back, and Boo emerged, soft and clean as ever.

"BOO!!!"

We laid Mazzy down in the crib and slipped that old cut-up tank top rag sewed by the Million Dollar Cleaners into her arms.

"Booooooooooooo."

And only THEN did everybody sleep.

Death Of A Blankie

When I created Mazzy's blankie out of two old tank tops, I never imagined my newborn would want to sleep with that item of clothing for the REST OF HER LIFE.

As Mazzy got older, her undying devotion to Boo just grew stronger. Boo helped put Mazzy to bed, assisted in spontaneous meltdown deflection, acted as her companion on family vacations, and generally encouraged a favorable disposition at all times.

Which was great!

Until Boo started dying.

You see—Mazzy loved Boo. But she did little to think of his well-being other than he must be on her person at all times. She dragged him on the floor, she threw him out of her stroller onto the city streets, and she chewed on him like he was a piece of rawhide. Since Boo was basically a makeshift sew job of two old rags, he was a goner from the get-go.

BLANKIE TIP #1: DO NOT CREATE A ONE-OF-A-KIND HOMEMADE BLANKIE.

Death started with a hole in the seam and quickly escalated into a complete unraveling of one entire side. Then holes started forming in places where seams didn't exist—a telltale sign the Blankie Reaper is near.

A plan to create a replacement Boo was born. I bought two soft T-shirts in contrasting shades of purple, just like the original. Then I cut them into squares and had them sewn by the tailor once again, creating possibly the most expensive rag known to man.

Harlow with Piggy, Doggy and Beary

Mazzy with Boo and her "brother" Henry

Mazzy loved it immediately though, and it became known as New Boo. But she was not ready to throw out her original Boo. Instead she renamed it Old Boo and carried both.

A year later, New Boo looked like he might disintegrate in the next load of laundry as well, so I purchased two more shirts and made another, urging Mazzy to love the Newest Boo just as much as all the others. Which she did, but that just meant a third companion was added to her VIB list. That's "Very Important Blankie," FYI.

Over the years, we had great success getting Mazzy to adopt new Boos. Unfortunately, we had less success convincing her to abandon the old Boos. She just added each new Boo to her growing stockpile and carried them around all at once.

Every time I thought we were getting close to a time in Mazzy's life when Boo(s) would be on his way out, something would happen and he would come back ten times stronger.

For instance, my cousin gave us a book called *Owen*, in which the title character has a blankie. Every time I took the book out to read it, Mazzy would throw it clear across the room, shouting, "NO! THAT'S A TERRIBLE BOOK!!!!"

After a few weeks of this, I mentioned it to my sister, because I thought it was funny that Mazzy was so vehemently against a book we had never read.

My sister laughed. "I read that book to Mazzy when you first got it. Do you know what it's about?"

"No. . . ."

"Owen has a blankie and everyone is suggesting ways for the parents to help him get rid of it. Finally, the mom cuts the blankie into pieces to sew

NAME:
BOO

OWNER:	MAZZY
YEARS IN USE:	6 YEARS
BACKSTORY:	AN OLD T-SHIRT SEWED INTO A BLANKIE
UPKEEP:	REPLICATED SEVEN TIMES, AND CURRENTLY CARRIED IN FOUR SEPARATE PIECES

them into his backpack. I guess Mazzy doesn't want you to get any ideas!"

And then it made perfect sense. Mazzy was right—I would have gotten some ideas.

The Unthinkable

In a surprising twist to this story (someone contact M. Night Shyamalan), at around the time she turned five, Mazzy suddenly decided she didn't need Original Boo anymore and threw it away. Only, she didn't tell Mike and me about her decision until later that same evening, after we had already sent the garbage down the chute of our building.

Now, here's the irony.

Mazzy was totally fine with the separation. No regrets. She told us offhandedly, hours after the fact, like it was no big deal. Why would it be a big deal to toss a dying rag?

Mike and I, however, were DEVASTATED.

"But . . . We should have saved it!"

"Why? It wasn't good anymore, Mom."

She was right. Original Boo was a shred of a shred of shred. And she still has several better, newer Boos.

But the one she threw out was the original. The first thing Mazzy slept with when we were too terrified to put anything but a sheet in her crib. The scrap of fabric she had cuddled since it was bigger than she was.

How could Mazzy have tossed her lifelong friend so unceremoniously???

I decided to take action. And by action, I mean dumpster diving.

I became convinced that we would find it. How many apartments were in the building? Not many. How much trash could they possibly accumulate? Everyone throws out their stuff in white kitchen bags, so I'd just have to identify which one was ours and go through that. How messy could it be?

I found out exactly how messy. I also found out most kitchen bags don't survive a trip down a garbage chute from several stories up.

IT WAS DISGUSTING.

We're talking fallen garbage mixed with other fallen garbage, that somehow looked like it had gotten soaked in a river. Who or what pours wet coffee grinds and gallons of orange juice directly down a garbage chute, I have no idea, but it's not pretty.

As I poked at one broken bag after the other and determined each was not fit to even touch, much less GO THROUGH, I realized Boo was gone. Mazzy was okay with it and I would have to be, too.

I let the loss of Boo settle, left for work, and moved on.

Later that evening, I returned home, and Ruth, our nanny, met me at the door.

"I have something to show you."

She led me into Mazzy's room and pulled a piece of Original Boo out of the back of the top drawer.

I had totally forgotten. When Boo first split in two, I had taken one half and put it in Mazzy's drawer for safekeeping. At the time, Boo was rapidly disintegrating, and putting half of it away seemed like a good way to double its life span. This was right before I decided to buy new T-shirts to make more Boos.

I took Original Boo out of Mazzy's drawer and transferred it to the back of my own drawer. Right next to my good jewelry and special cards I keep from Mike.

A few days later, when Mazzy decided yet another Boo could be trashed, I took that Boo and put it in the back of my drawer, too.

They are still there to this day. Now I'm the one stockpiling rags.

Mazzy might be realizing she is getting too old for her blankie.

But that doesn't mean I'm ready to let my baby go.

CHAPTER 18

Give Me Back My iPad

There are people who say you shouldn't let your kids watch TV until they are two, but those people are out of their goddamn minds and DO NOT LISTEN TO THEM. We tried to keep Mazzy away from the television when she was little but then our sitter started showing her *Sesame Street* videos on YouTube, which appeared to be teaching her the alphabet and how to count to ten (in SPANISH, mind you), and then it was like—well, maybe TV is actually more qualified to parent than we are. . . . Let's just say, it's all a slippery slope from there.

Of course, there are positives and negatives to owning a device with the power to stop the whining, end a tantrum, and cure boredom all with the press of a button.

Wait. What's the negative again?

Oh, yeah. You can't pretend to be better than your mom friends because you alone possess the power to control your kid without a handheld device.

We tend to limit screen time to the mornings because my kids wake up really early and there is a hard stop when the kids have to go to school. Yes, there is some whining and negotiating to put the damn things away so they can get dressed, but for the most part, the screens allow Mike and me time to get ready ourselves while the kids are occupied.

We don't let the kids have screen time in the evening (except for Friday Movie Night) because I've heard screen time can make it hard for kids to fall asleep afterward, and as I've written back in chapter 8, we don't need any more trouble in that department.

Sometimes on a random weekend or on vacation, our screen limits relax and we all sit on the couch as a family, staring at our assorted screens. I'm sure it would look like absolutely horrific parenting from an outsider's perspective, but a few moments of everyone relaxing together on the couch in their own little bubbles is actually a really enjoyable experience.

I highly recommend partaking sometime, as long as you can do it guilt-free.

The Next YouTube Generation

Originally, I thought time spent on the iPad was better than time spent watching TV, because iPads are interactive. Then one day, Mazzy was watching *Sesame Street* on YouTube and clicked on a seemingly innocent Elmo video on the adjacent sidebar, which ended up being someone pouring gasoline on Elmo and lighting him on fire.

Yep, one minute Elmo was making small talk with his goldfish and the next his body parts were burning and flying through the air.

There was also the time Mazzy was watching Barney, and I found myself lunging across the living room when Bart Simpson showed up, pulled an assault rifle on Barney, and gunned him down in cold cartoon dinosaur blood.

Not exactly an image you want your baby remembering from their childhood.

This was in ancient times, before the app YouTube Kids was invented, so maybe this problem has already been solved. But they can still easily navigate to those ladies opening toys and surprise eggs. Do you know those women make millions of dollars a year? Our generation has dedicated our lives to circumventing ads on TV, and as payback, our kids are choosing to watch ten-minute-long toy commercials back-to-back-to-back on our iPads. And using up all our battery life in the process.

I'm convinced that most people earning a large income on YouTube are people who have figured out what's appealing to toddlers.

So I guess you have to weigh the interactivity of an iPad with the full control you have over what your kids are watching on TV. Is passively viewing *Sofia the First* on TV better than navigating to a video of someone opening a *Sofia the First* toy on YouTube? Probably.

Sometimes I now find myself forcing the kids to watch television because I know Daniel Tiger is teaching about feelings and My Little Pony is espousing the virtues of friendship and Team Umizoomi is explaining basic math skills, whereas I have no idea what the forty-year-old woman playing with *Frozen* dolls is teaching.

I do like when Mazzy and Harlow watch cooking and baking tutorials on YouTube (which they love), because I imagine that one day, I might be able to sit on the couch while they make me dinner.

Even better, maybe they'll make their own baking tutorials, become huge YouTube stars, and then pay for their own college educations.

That's my very modern dream.

I find it hilarious how much we shielded Mazzy from television as a newborn—like it would poison her brain so that it would never rise above a *Bubble Guppies* comprehension level. If that's the case, then my second child is screwed because she was exposed to television straight from the womb. Harlow went from watching the inside of my uterus to sliding out the birth canal and landing on a couch with *PAW Patrol* playing on repeat.

It's impossible to stop your second child from watching television when your older already knows how to work the remote. Not only work the remote, but change the video format from cable to Apple TV so she can switch to Netflix.

I don't even know how to do that.

Smartphone Problems Only Parents Understand

Kids of all ages can wreck your phone. At one year old, they can throw your iPhone in the toilet and at four years old they can waste your battery talking to Siri. She answers questions and will even tell Mazzy a story if she asks nicely. Don't believe me? Ask Siri to tell you a story. She'll try to get out of it, but if you let her know you won't stop asking until she obliges (sounds like parenting!), she's got quite a tale to tell you.

When your child is six years old, that's when things get really interesting. Mazzy's friend Gavin got ahold of my phone the other day and told Siri to call him Gavin. Do you know what happened? Siri switched everything—my contact info, my email nickname, and even the name of my AirDrop to "Gavin." I couldn't figure out what was going on until I realized I'd been pranked by a tech-savvy six-year-old.

I wasn't pissed. I was impressed.

Here are six more problems you'll have if you share your smart phone with your child:

WHEN YOUR TODDLER FINALLY HANDS OVER YOUR IPHONE.

iPhone is disabled

try again in 45 minutes

WHEN YOU LET YOUR TODDLER USE YOUR PHONE AND THINK,

WHAT'S THE WORST THAT CAN HAPPEN?

WHEN YOU RUN OUT OF STORAGE ON YOUR PHONE AND YOU LOOK THROUGH YOUR PHOTOS TO FIGURE OUT WHY.

WHEN YOUR BABY TAKES HER FIRST STEPS AND YOU GRAB YOUR PHONE SO YOU CAN RECORD THE MOMENT AND REMEMBER IT FOREVER.

WHEN YOU GIVE YOUR TODDLER YOUR PHONE AND SHE GIVES IT BACK WITH ONE APP MISSING

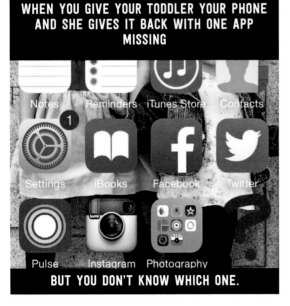

BUT YOU DON'T KNOW WHICH ONE.

WHEN YOUR KID LEARNS HOW TO POST PICTURES ON FACEBOOK.

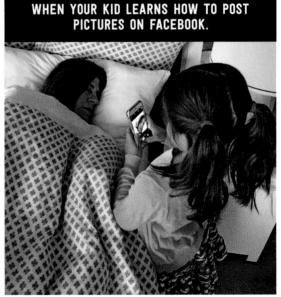

Toddlers On Facebook

If toddlers were allowed to join Facebook, can you imagine what they would say about you online?

 Mazzy W
3 minutes

My mom thinks I'm going down for a nap when we get home. BWAHAHA. She's hilarious.

15 Toddlers like this

 Arami R I DON'T WANNA NAP EITHER!!!!!
Like · Reply · 👍 3 · 2 minutes

 Neve B FYI, I convinced my mom I don't need a nap. Now she lets me watch TV every afternoon because SHE needs a break. WIN!
Like · Reply · 👍 3 · 1 minutes

 Sydney B
7 minutes

I pooped in the bath last night and my mom had to scoop it up with a cup and flush it down the toilet. LMAO!

21 Toddlers like this

 Ella B I hope it wasn't one of my sippy cups, sis!
Like · Reply · 👍 2 · 2 minutes

 Luke K
10 minutes

Forgot the teacher's name at Gymboree today so I called her 'Mommy'. What's the big deal? Isn't that every woman's name?

15 Toddlers like this

 Giles G It's the woman's name at my house.
Like · Reply · 👍 3 · 9 minutes

 Mazzy W Mine too!
Like · Reply · 👍 3 · 12 minutes

 Gavin K
17 minutes

So, here's the thing. I totally know how to use the potty. But mommy keeps giving me treats if I make it seem like a surprise when I go. Psht. Diapers for life, yo.

47 Toddlers like this

 Madeline W I stopped using diapers at 15 months.
Like · Reply · 15 minutes

Jake K ^^ Unlike.
Like · Reply · 👍 32 · 11 minutes

 Matt K
18 minutes

I opened all of my mom's tampons today and watched them expand in the toilet. It was awesome. You should all try this at home.

16 Toddlers like this

 Jack B
24 minutes

Why did Mommy walk into the laundry room?? Oh no, I don't think she is ever coming back! I'm going to be in the living room alone FOREVER!!!!!!!

1 Toddler likes this

 Jack B UPDATE: She came back. Sorry for the false alarm.
Like · Reply · 👍 2 · 23 minutes

 Harlow W
25 minutes

It's fun to ask for "no bubbles" once my bubble bath is ready.

18 Toddlers like this

 Zoe G
32 minutes

Is it bedtime yet? Because that's the time I like to announce it's time to eat my dinner.

10 Toddlers likes this

 Madeline W I'm about to pretend I need to poop on the potty so...YES.
Like · Reply · 👍 15 · 12 minutes

 Jake G
36 minutes

My cat really looks like he needs his tail pulled. Repeatedly.

34 Toddlers like this

 Tyler W
48 minutes

Watch, I'm gonna ask for a red popsicle and when my mom gives it to me, I'm going to scream "I SAID PURPLE" and have a fit.

84 Toddlers like this

 Jed B Ha! I tried that yesterday with the blue sippy cup instead of the green one. SO MUCH FUN!
Like · Reply · 👍 18 · 44 minutes

 Charlie G LOL. Moms are so easy to piss off.
Like · Reply · 👍 24 · 18 minutes

TODDLERS ON INSTAGRAM

Toddlers might not be allowed on Facebook, but I know at least one toddler who is on Instagram. No, for real. Look up @insta2yearold. It's Harlow.

insta2yearold   37w

♥ 4,838 likes

insta2yearold I'd hate to be an adult. All that walking must cut into their nap time. #strollerlife #zzzzzzzzzzzz

insta2yearold   12w

♥ 4,163 likes

insta2yearold Say what you will about my mom's cooking skills but she can defrost one helluva waffle.

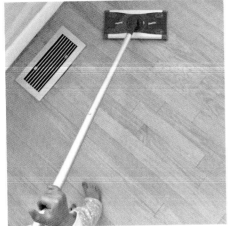

♥ 4,838 likes

insta2yearold My mom suggested we play Cinderella which sounded awesome at first... but now I'm beginning to question her motivation. #childlabor

♥ 4,198 likes

insta2yearold My mom always complains about year-old magazines in the doctor's office. Well, this book is from 1947. #iwin #pediatrician

♥ 4,679 likes

insta2yearold I told my mom I drew a castle and she said, "WOW! That's amazing!!!" I know it's scribble. I just like to mess with her.

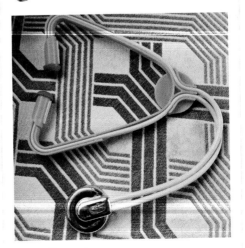

♥ 4,118 likes

insta2yearold I'm not sure how to break it to them but I just discovered nobody in my family has a heartbeat. #iseedeadpeople

CHAPTER 19

Traveling With Kids

There's getting there and there's being there, and as they say, getting there is half the battle. Or is it half the fun? In this scenario, it's a battle. There is nothing fun about traveling with kids.

Traveling with babies is like everything else—it depends on the baby. You may get lucky and have a child who will sleep twenty-four hours to China or you might have a baby who treats three hours to Florida like you're shipping him off to army camp.

All I know is that you will pack up your entire house, and possibly the house next door, before you leave, momentarily forgetting that diapers and wipes are not sold exclusively in your hometown.

Let's start with road trips, because that seems a little less daunting than plane travel. After all, you can pull over, get out of the car, and scream out your frustration on the side of the highway if necessary. If you are the only adult in the car, then you've got your work cut out for you. And by that I mean—you must ignore your crying, whining children, or else you aren't going ANYWHERE.

One thing I learned while driving three-month-old Mazzy on an hour-long journey by myself was that stopping to tend to your crying baby only delays the inevitable. At some point you are going to have to strap her into that car seat and drive, whether she is screaming or not.

> If I ever get PTSD, the trigger will be the dinging sound that the seat belt makes when you have to take it off while the car is moving.

Passenger Vs. Driver

Remember when being the passenger was the easy job? The person who got to sleep while the driver was the hero who got everyone where they needed to go?

I used to LOVE road trips. Mainly because I am excellent at falling asleep in a car. At my old job, it was a running joke that although I had traveled the half hour to our client in New Jersey about ten thousand times, I would not be able to tell anyone how to get there because I had never once made the trip fully awake. I can fall asleep on a five-minute drive. It's quite a gift.

At least it was a gift. Now the fact that being on the road makes me sleepy is definitely to

my disadvantage, because this is precisely the moment I have to be 100 percent on my mom game. While everyone else stays safely buckled in their seats, the passenger is required to remove their own seat belt at least fifty times per trip, as she contorts her body like she's part of a Chinese circus act to fetch lost pacifiers, locate snacks at the bottom of the snack bag, and even switch seamlessly from the front to the backseat while the vehicle is moving, in order to soothe crying babies to sleep.

If I ever get PTSD, the trigger will be the dinging sound that the seat belt makes when you have to take it off while the car is moving.

A little car trip shut-eye is a concept that no longer computes.

In fact, sometimes, in particularly bad circumstances, shotgun eludes the passenger entirely and he/she must sit shoved between car seats in the back, feeding a bottle to a baby while playing games with a three-year-old at the same time.

On one road trip, I remember singing "You Are My Sunshine" to a crying Harlow (it's the only thing that guaranteed a smile) while pretending to be a shark and bite Mazzy so she wouldn't get mad that my attention was diverted from her.

"You are my sun CHOMP, my only sun CHOMP, you make me hap-CHOMP, when skies are gray CHOMP CHOMP CHOMP . . ."

I was playing two different audiences at the same time. Impressive stuff.

As for the driver?

His vacation had already started.

PARENTAL RESPONSIBILITIES ON A FAMILY ROAD TRIP

DRIVER:	PASSENGER:
Stay awake, drive.	Field snack requests, find and distribute snacks, clean up after snacks, monitor electronic usage and battery power, fetch lost pacifiers, locate hiding lovies, find very specific toys, retrieve items after they have been purposefully dropped on the floor, risk life and limb by jumping back and forth between the back and front seats, entertain with endless stream of songs and games, check for dirty diapers, feed bottles, negotiate battles between siblings, remove shoes and sweaters, rummage through backseat for random requests from driver, google questions asked by driver on mobile device, read directions, look out for rest stops and bathrooms, monitor song selection, sing lullabies to crying babies, soothe children to sleep, talk down tantruming toddlers, distract kids from misery of being strapped in carseat for extended period of time, maintain health and happiness of everyone in car by sacrificing own emotional well-being.

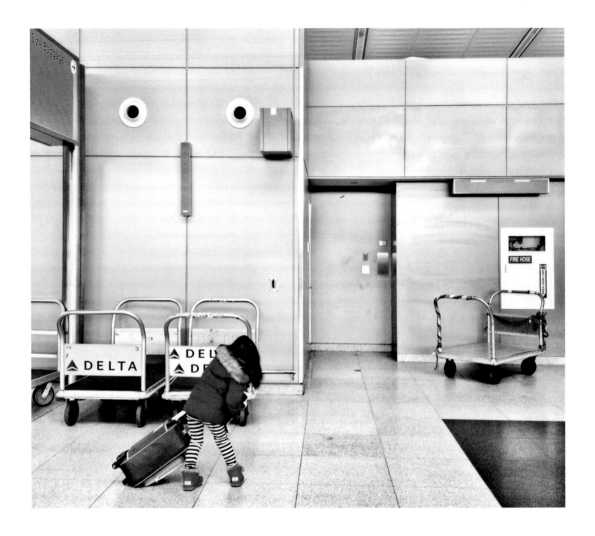

When You Have To Catch A Plane

Before you catch a plane, you have to get out your front door. This task is hard enough without a flight to catch, which is why moms are notoriously late for everything. We have built-in excuses that came out of our vaginas.

"I'm so sorry—I just couldn't get Brian out the door."

"I tried to get here on time but Ella refused to put her shoes on and, well, you know how it goes."

For the most part, people are understanding. Or at least they pretend to be to our faces.

But you know who couldn't give a shit about Ella's shoe aversion? American Airlines. Or Delta. Or Virgin. Or whatever airline you booked that knows their entire passenger list will be much happier if your baby misses their flight.

Mike and I are both at our worst when we are trying to make a plane. We were this way even before kids. I am constantly running back in a panic for items I realize I forgot after we are already in the car, which drives my husband OUT OF HIS MIND, because he was packed and ready to go three days ago.

Me:

"Oh wait! I need a bathing suit for the hot tub!"

"Crap! I forgot sunglasses!"

"Oh no! I have no snacks!"

Mike:

"THIS IS THE LAST TIME I TRAVEL WITH YOU!!!!!!!!!!!"

Of course, with kids, this is all happening while we are dressing two complete invalids who are exhausted and have no idea what is going on.

"CAN YOU CHECK IF I PUT A BOTTLE IN THE DIAPER BAG?"

"DON'T YOU SEE ME PUTTING ON HARLOW'S SHOES?"

"WELL, I CAN'T DO IT IF I'M BRUSHING MAZZY'S HAIR!!!"

We have a level of panic and urgency like the neighborhood is being invaded and we have to get out with our lives on our backs because we might never be able to return.

In reality, we are off to a family ski trip in Utah.

The Trouble With The Airport

We all know the plane is too small to contain the energy of a toddler, but it would be a grave mistake to underestimate the obstacle of the airport terminal—a place that presents small children with limitless possibilities and opportunities for escape.

There's a wide hallway the length of several football fields, moving sidewalks, ramps, and various stores from which to steal random merchandise.

Add all this to the fact that, in addition to your children, you are responsible for lugging all your baggage . . . Well. You are in for an exciting parenting challenge!

> Mazzy looked at JFK Airport like her personal playground. I watched her eyes go wild as she contemplated where to go next.

When Harlow was around fifteen months, we traveled with her in a car-seat stroller up until security, where you have to somehow dismantle all your belongings, undress, and hold on to your children at the same time. After security, Harlow threw a fit when I tried to put her back in the stroller, so I decided to let her walk, since she was about to spend the next five hours sitting on my lap with nowhere to go.

Unfortunately, Harlow looked at the airport as her ticket to freedom. She refused to hold anybody's hand and took off at full speed, heading in the opposite direction of our gate, like she had an international flight to catch and had no time for our domestic excursion.

Mazzy looked at JFK airport like her personal playground. I watched her eyes go wild as she contemplated where to go next. Along with the sprawling space, there is also endless temptation. Mazzy tried to walk off with a very elaborate M&M's container from the duty-free shop and in the time it took me to put it back, Harlow ran up to Hudson News, stole three PowerBars, and ran back out.

One time, when Mazzy was younger, I had brought her with me inside a stall in the airport bathroom. While I was peeing, she crawled under the stall door and ran straight out of the ladies' room! I could barely get my pants up before I had to chase after her. Plus, in the interest of saving my daughter from mistakenly boarding a flight to Moscow, I abandoned my carry-on in the john.

Don't tell the TSA.

THE RANGE OF EMOTIONS ONE EXPERIENCES WHEN BRINGING A BABY ON A PLANE

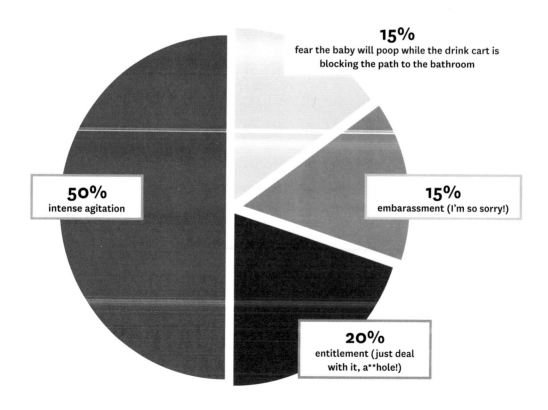

15%
fear the baby will poop while the drink cart is blocking the path to the bathroom

50%
intense agitation

15%
embarassment (I'm so sorry!)

20%
entitlement (just deal with it, a**hole!)

Babies On A Plane Are Scarier Than Snakes

The first thing to understand about plane travel is that if your baby starts crying, all the other passengers will HATE YOU. Which is especially unsettling if you are a people pleaser like me. Parents flying with babies are the pariahs of the air. Boarding a plane with a baby is like announcing you hate Justin Bieber on Twitter. As you walk down that aisle, everyone is praying you are not sitting near them.

However, sometimes you think your baby is annoying everybody when really it's just you. I

spent an entire flight (in a middle seat, mind you), trying to get Mazzy to sit still on my lap. I was shushing, rocking, and bouncing, desperately hoping she would fall asleep, which

never happened. I thought I was going through hell and that everyone in close proximity was mentally crossing off "Have Baby" from their to-do list. But when the plane landed, they all commented on how well-behaved she was. I think passengers notice crying but not much else. As long as your child isn't interrupting their in-flight movie, she's your problem and yours alone.

As your kid gets a little older, some of these issues will go away while new, harder issues arise. I'm sorry to break it to you, but traveling with toddlers is way harder than traveling with babies.

Toddlers don't sleep, they get bored easily, spill things, lose their toys between the seat cushions, kick the seat in front of them (that's a way to get to know your neighbors fast!), and will reject every snack you packed in your carry-on. That's a fact.

"I'm hungry."

"Do you want pretzels?"

"No."

"Mini carrots?"

"No."

"Dried mango?"

"No."

"Almonds?"

"No."

"Apple squeezie?"

"No."

"Animal crackers?"

"No."

It's like they think you'll suddenly remember the side pocket of your carry-on has a mini oven, where you can bake a cake using invisible ingredients found in your wallet.

Plus, toddlers do not understand why they need to stay strapped in their seats.

On a flight when Harlow was about fifteen months, she acted like sitting in my lap was a death sentence and wanted nothing more than to run up and down the aisle, checking out what everybody was doing on their laptops. She'd casually rest her hand on each person's knee as she peered at their Excel spread sheets and their videos of *The Hangover*. I pretended that every-one thought the intrusion was adorable and didn't try to stop her.

Finally, we got reprimanded by a flight atten-dant to go back to our seats—a small price to pay for five minutes of toddler freedom. At least Har-low provided entertainment value for the passen-gers when she ran in the opposite direction and then threw a fit when I stopped her from running straight though the curtain into first class.

Tell me about it, Harlow. Tell me about it.

During hour two, Harlow became incredibly overtired but refused to relax, no matter how inviting we tried to arrange the airline blanket across our laps. She cried and squealed and was truly miserable. The only thing we could do to calm her down was take turns holding her while pacing the aisle.

"Look at us! We can't even control a small child! We're obviously regretting our parenting choices—particularly the one to take her on this vacation. Yes, vacation! Isn't that HILARIOUS????"

Judging by the way she was trying to writhe her way out of our arms, half the people on the plane probably thought we were kidnapping her from her real parents.

Mike finally got her to fall asleep around hour three, which was exactly the same time she

Look at us! We can't even control a small child! We're obviously regretting our parenting choices— particularly the one to take her on this vacation.

unloaded in her diaper. Then we were faced with the decision to change her and risk waking her up or to let her be and deal with the stench.

We opted to change her. Do I have to remind you how small plane bathroom changing tables are? It's like they were built for preemies who were born without legs.

Harlow was so exhausted and fell back asleep as soon as the diaper change was complete. Time for everyone to relax, right?

WRONG. The was precisely the moment Mazzy decided she had nothing left to watch on her iPad.

Ah, yes—if you think traveling with one child is hard, wait until you travel with TWO.

Preschoolers On A Plane Are Where It's At

If you are traveling with a baby or a toddler, you have so much gear, the chances of avoiding baggage check are less than zero. If you are traveling with a preschooler, you put some clothes in a suitcase, just like she's a regular person. You load an iPad with games and movies, pack a few portable entertainment items (like paper and crayons), and then you are on your way. Not only can they drag their own suitcase, they're even excited to do it. But that doesn't mean it's without its fair share of obstacles and irritations.

Here are twelve things you should know before traveling with a preschooler on a plane:

1. Preschoolers need to be informed of every aspect of the trip ahead of time. I told Mazzy we were flying to the Dominican Republic. Then she nearly flipped when she realized the plane was not picking us up directly in front of our apartment. Ditto for landing. I think Mazzy expected to walk straight from the runway to the beach. A twenty-minute shuttle can be torturous for the unprepared.

2. Explain to your preschooler that there will be a full day for travel. After we arrived at the hotel, checked in, and got settled, Mazzy took one look out the window and started crying. "IT'S DARK OUT!!!!" "I know, babe. It's bedtime soon." "I THOUGHT WE WERE GOING TO THE BEACH!!!!!!!" "We're going to the beach tomorrow." "NOOOOOOOOOO!!!!!!!!" Oops.

3. Your child might be really excited to see the ground get smaller and smaller during takeoff. But, be aware, once she is safely buckled in, she may be too short to see anything but bright blue sky. "I CAN'T SEE IT!!!!!!" she'll wail as you point out tiny cars and bird's-eye views of pools and baseball stadiums. Just keep quiet, cut your losses, and give her the middle seat from the get-go. There's always next year.

4. If you put headphones on your four-year-old, make sure they fit because there is nothing more annoying than holding the headphones on your child's head for the entirety of the flight. Also be forewarned, wearing headphones means your child will make all her normal demands except 100 times louder. If you've ever heard a booming voice asking for apple juice from up above, that was not God getting thirsty. That was a preschooler on a plane.

5. If you are excited to leave the stroller at home, please be aware that your child could pass out on the way to the airport for your return flight. After all, she's exhausted at the end of her vacation. I had to carry Mazzy's lifeless thirty-six-pound body all through baggage check, while waiting on the ridiculously long security line, and through customs, while Mike somehow handled all six of our bags by himself.

6. Pack light. Your child might be gung ho to carry her own suitcase when you leave the house, but I guarantee that enthusiasm will wane by the return flight home.

7. Try to find that sweet spot between rushing to the plane and allowing yourself too much time in the airport. The last thing you want is to use up all your snacks and cures for boredom before you've even left the ground. Plus, that precious iPad battery time is your most valuable commodity.

8. Charge, charge some more, and then charge again.

9. Be prepared to spend a good hour of your trip searching for lost toys and crayons. You might want to wear pants that show minimal butt crack, since your ass will be hanging out in the aisle while you crawl under the seats.

10. On many airlines, the TV controls are located right on top of the armrest. Those buttons are hard to resist even if your child has been warned that they'll change the channel,

lower the volume, or god forbid take them away from their regularly scheduled programming straight to the map. "MOM!!!!! WHAT HAPPENED TO MY SHOW?????!!!!!!"

11. Advanced motor skills are a wonderful thing. Until it means your child can now unbuckle her seat belt by herself.

12. You know how the person who gets from the plane to customs the fastest gets to the head of the line and then goes home the fastest? TELL YOUR CHILD THAT. When we flew back into New York at nine p.m., Mazzy was exhausted and looked like she might fall over at any moment. But when we told her the path to customs was literally a race? I have never seen anyone move faster. The kicker? When we arrived toward the front of the pack, she screamed, "I WIN!!!!!!!" Big laughs all around.

The Light At The End Of The Tunnel

When Harlow was almost three and Mazzy was almost six, we took them on a three-hour plane ride. I have to say—they were both fantastic. They didn't try to run away from us in the airport, they talked and played with each other on the plane, they were excited to have unlimited access to their iPads, and they ate what they were given. They were particularly excited to get free snacks delivered directly to their seats.

As the plane took off, Mazzy turned to Harlow excitedly and said, "Harlow—we're taking off!" Harlow looked out the window as the plane left the ground and shouted, "We're up in the sky!!!!"

Then the two of them giggled and smiled before promptly turning back to their iPads.

It was a really smooth trip. Toward the end, even the surrounding passengers remarked on how awesome my kids had behaved throughout the flight. I was so proud.

Then the plane touched down, Harlow threw up in my lap, and everyone around us wanted to die.

CHAPTER 20

Even Ice Cream Causes Tantrums

Parents can't win. Little kids don't appreciate any-thing and it doesn't matter what you give them, they will always want more. One of the hardest things in life is feeling underappreciated. Unfortunately for you, that's what parenting is ALL ABOUT.

Every time I give Mazzy something special (a cookie, a present, etc.) she ends up asking for another one. It's like nothing ends until there are tears, whether I say "Yes" right off the bat or three chocolate-covered Oreo cookies later.

You got your kid a toy? He wanted a bigger one. You said your kid could watch a show? She'll want a second show. You bought her a cup of ice cream? She wanted a cone! You made him put on a jacket before he left the house? YOU MONSTER.

First-World Problems: Preschool Edition

The thing that is so hard about your kids falling lifeless on the floor in a puddle of spit and tears is that they have it SO GOOD. They have every commercial-free episode of *PAW Patrol* available for free at the tap of a button. They have blocks and puzzles falling out of their ears. They have the rapt attention of two grown adults willing to dress them, bathe them, and rock them to sleep.

Kids will ha ve meltdowns over everything, from the disappearance of their favorite sippy cup to putting on their own shoes.

Is it easier to put your five-year-old's shoes on so you can all get out the door on time? Of course. But then thirteen years later when your eighteen-year-old asks her college roommate to tie her shoelaces and the roommate refuses and your kid is left sitting alone in her dorm room because she can't go to class in bare feet, which eventually leads to her flunking out of college—that's on you.

Ninety-nine percent of parenting is not doing what is easiest for the short-term result. You need to think about your end game. If we constantly give in, our tiny tyrants will control us for the rest of our lives.

I'm not going to lie. Choosing long-term lessons over keeping the peace is the hardest part of parenting. I failed just this morning. Sometimes you need to stop the crying to save your own sanity.

That's OK, too.

WHEN YOUR KID HATES NEW YORK

The Wrath Of Harlow

Harlow is the kind of kid who flips out over the littlest of things. She likes her waffle cut a certain way and her water delivered to her with the straw facing outward. She wants to hold your arm when you pour the milk into her cereal and if you forget, she will unleash an anger so acute you'd think she just witnessed the brutal killing of her puppy.

She is also a neat freak. She's the only kid I know who can eat an entire ice cream cone and not get any on her clothes. But this also means that if she spills a smidgen of milk outside her cereal bowl or gets a drop of frosting on her chin, all hell breaks loose. The kid uses more napkins on a daily basis than a BBQ joint. If the EPA ever wanted to truly save some forests, all they'd have to do is cut off Harlow's access to paper products.

Harlow's anger can turn on a dime, too. The other day, it was raining and Harlow got excited to jump in the puddles. She took one big jump, laughing as the water sprayed up around her. Then she burst into tears because her pants got wet.

If Harlow isn't freaking out about getting dirty (which is as frustrating as it is adorable), it's usually because she is tired or hungry or both. Although, she never realizes this on her own. I spend much of Harlow's tantrums trying to convince her to have something to eat, which is harder than it sounds.

The calm usually comes soon after she takes that first bite.

My recommendation is to have snacks on hand whenever there is a tantrum. If your kid is crying about a crack in the sidewalk, sometimes eating

HARLOW (VS) HARLOW

a cheese stick might make her realize she's not so mad at the sidewalk after all.

The best feeling is when you've finally got your Mr. Hyde back to Dr. Jekyll. Once Harlow is fed or has napped or has taken a bath (washing off any foreign substances she encountered throughout the day), the smile returns, my snuggler is back, and the show goes on.

My recommendation is to have snacks on hand whenever there is a tantrum.

EVERY GOOD KID TOYS WITH THE DARK SIDE

AUSTIN **VS** AUSTIN

MAIA **VS** MAIA

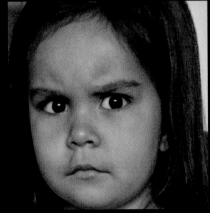

LYLE VS LYLE

PIPER VS PIPER

CHARLIE VS CHARLIE

EMILIA VS EMILIA

AURORA VS AURORA

NICHOLAS VS NICHOLAS

Are Vacations Really Vacations?

Tantrums aren't just relegated to regular days—kids plant seeds of discontent on special occasions, too.

Vacations with babies are really not vacations at all. It's just doing all the same stuff you usually do, except less conveniently. Babies have rituals and routines at home that are in place for a reason—to make the day go as smoothly and as predictably as possible. If you take your baby off his schedule and give him a bunch of surprises (even if that surprise is beachfront property), you are opening yourself up to all kinds of disasters.

Our first trip with Mazzy was when she was three months old. We took her to Miami for a weekend and spent the majority of the time locked in a dark hotel room trying not to breathe so she would stick to her napping schedule. This meant Mike and I had to lay very still on the bed, watching movies on our iPhones with separate headphones, while it was eighty degrees and beautiful just outside.

Mike and I both love to travel and always thought we would be the kind of parents who wouldn't think twice about taking our baby with us on a trip. But sometimes things do not depend on the wants of the parents, it depends on the needs of the baby.

After taking Mazzy on several short weekend trips her first year, one thing became clear. She did not share our travel gene. At least not yet.

When we were house guests, most often we would all have to share a room. Mazzy found it impossible to go to sleep knowing we were lying right next to her, available for play. Even if we got her down successfully at her bedtime, when Mike and I went to bed a few hours later, Mazzy seemed to have a Baby Google Alert on our reentry into the room. And she'd done her research, because she seemed to know we wouldn't let her cry it out because we feared never getting invited back.

In both cases, I was left with no choice but to pick her up and hold her until morning as she stared at me with confused saucer-sized eyes and exasperated tears streaming down her tiny little face.

If she could talk, she would be asking, "WHY ARE WE HERE???"

I had to admit—I didn't know, either.

Even if the day went well while we were away, around dinnertime I would start dreading the night. We finally came to the conclusion that going away wasn't worth it and opted to stay home.

There were tears. There was screaming. In tropical weather, which should be against the law.

When Mazzy was four, we took her to the Dominican Republic. That turned out to be the right age for her to appreciate a vacation. Well, not ANY vacation—a beach resort. Four-year-olds can definitely appreciate summer during winter. IT BLEW MAZZY'S MIND.

"It feels like summer here!!!!"

"It always feels like summer here!"

"Why don't we live here?"

"You know, that's a really good question."

With a four-year-old, we were no longer bound to a napping schedule, but that still didn't mean we got to do what we wanted to do. Which was RELAXING. There would be no relaxing at all. With a kid, the majority of your beach vacation is spent making sure nobody drowns, rather than napping poolside.

Mazzy wanted to be in the pool at all times, and since she was just learning how to swim, I had to be in there with her. There was no testing the water, acclimating to the temperature, and then taking my sweet time before I fully submerged myself, as I had been doing my entire life. If your kid jumps right in, you have to do the same.

There were several pools on the property and Mazzy wanted to swim in all of them. She'd jump in one pool and I'd have to quickly undress and

jump in, too. Then five minutes later, she'd be out and running to test out another pool and I'd have to grab our stuff, run after her, and jump in all over again.

I can't tell you how many abandoned drinks I left in our wake.

At one point, I dared to suggest that we remain at one pool for the rest of the afternoon. What do you think happened?

"NOOOOOOOOOOOOOOOOOOOO!!!!!!!!!!!"

There were tears. There was screaming. In tropical weather, which should be against the law.

"Mazzy, if you don't stop screaming, then we will have to go back to the room."

Then I got worried because I didn't want to go back to the room either but, obviously, you never want to deliver an empty threat. So there's another lesson for you: Don't ever threaten something if you don't intend to follow through. My husband always does this.

"If you don't stop crying, we are not going to Grammy's for Thanksgiving!"

I give him a look because OF COURSE we are going to Grammy's for Thanksgiving.

Luckily, on that day by the pool in the Dominican Republic, Mazzy stopped crying and I didn't have to sacrifice the entire day. But I also realized it was my fault she had gotten upset to begin with. Mazzy was thrilled to be there and wanted to experience all the pools and I had rained on her parade.

I just had to accept that vacations are different now. They can be lots of fun. But they are definitely not relaxing. Especially when there are bodies of water involved.

Somewhere into the third day, after twenty pool hops and screaming, "IT'S SUMMER HERE!!!!!" to

TAKING A TODDLER TO THE BEACH IS . . .

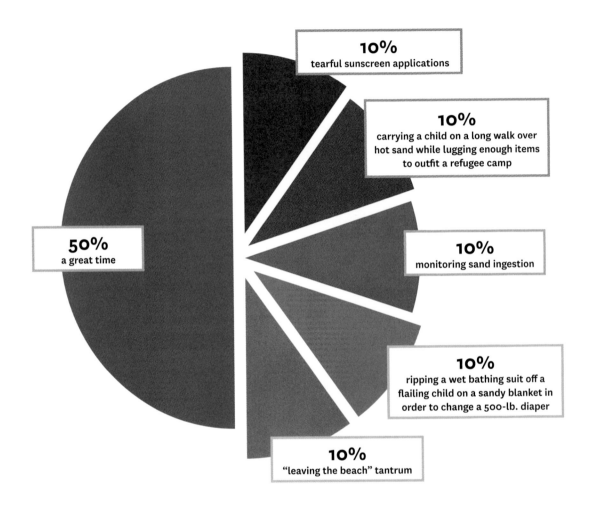

10%
tearful sunscreen applications

10%
carrying a child on a long walk over hot sand while lugging enough items to outfit a refugee camp

50%
a great time

10%
monitoring sand ingestion

10%
ripping a wet bathing suit off a flailing child on a sandy blanket in order to change a 500-lb. diaper

10%
"leaving the beach" tantrum

anyone who would listen, Mazzy crawled into my lap and cuddled with me briefly on a lounge chair.

"Thank you, Mom, for all of this."

Oh, my heart.

Where did my whining, entitled four-year-old go?

No worries! She was waiting for me at baggage claim as soon as we returned to New York.

CHAPTER 21 # Bragging Rights

Mazzy and Harlow were both early developers and I spent a good deal of time quite certain they were legit geniuses. I bragged about them on my blog in a joking fashion, but if I'm honest, I was serious. I imagined Mazzy was one of those crazy-smart kids who would graduate ten years early with a full scholarship to Harvard. Just because she could stack three blocks earlier than most.

It took me a few years before I realized rolling over early is not always a prerequisite for being president. And being able to pick up a Cheerio with two fingers is something all babies do, not just future CEOs.

All moms associate minor acts with amazingness. We don't realize how ridiculous we sound until we hear other people do it. And even then, we still think we're justified with our own kids.

This is why your Facebook feed is filled with inane things like . . .

"Charlie pulled up to standing. Next stop—THE OLYMPICS!!!"

Bragging about our kids is a god-given right.

Have you ever mentioned your kids' accomplishments to a group of moms without having them offer up their kids' own accomplishments in return? I do it, too. I hear myself and I'm like—SHUT UP, ILANA, THIS ISN'T ABOUT YOUR KID. But I can't help myself. I think it's a natural reflex to be like "Oh yeah? Your toddler builds high towers? Well, mine is excellent at puzzles!"

I don't think it ever ends, which is precisely why my mother always insists I go to temple for Rosh Hashanah back in my hometown. So she can show off her middle-aged daughter to her friends.

The Maybe Baby Model

I was approached by a modeling scout for Mazzy when she was around a year old. Having never been approached by a modeling scout myself (I'm five-four with a faint mustache), I didn't realize stuff like that actually happened. I was flattered, took her in, and got her signed to an agency. Next thing I knew, Mazzy and I were at a casting call for a major diaper brand. They were looking for babies to put on the package.

There were dozens of babies in a holding room, some crawling around and some clinging to their parents while their shifty-eyed moms and dads checked out the competition. It seemed like a long shot, but Mazzy was just as adorable as the next baby, and she had no issues with separation anxiety, which turned out to be a huge plus. Each kid had to be taken into a separate room for the actual audition while the parents stayed behind. Mazzy was led into the other room by a stranger with no qualms whatsoever, which was both awesome and semi-disturbing. I tried my best to look sympathetic when another mom tried to hand her baby over to the stranger and the baby burst into tears.

Guess your one-year-old doesn't have what it takes, lady!

"What it takes" being the inability to differentiate between the arms of a casting agent and the loving arms of one's own mother.

Later that day, we got a call from the agency. Mazzy was chosen. I'm not even going to try to downplay my excitement. Can you imagine better bragging rights than having your baby on the package of a major diaper brand?

There was one catch. Being chosen for the shoot didn't guarantee Mazzy's picture would actually be used. They would be shooting three babies but only using two. We wouldn't know who until after they assessed the photos.

On shoot day, everyone ooohed and aaahed over Mazzy like she was the next Kendall Jenner and I got to congratulate myself on my offspring's clearly superior genes. My mustache and I were so, so smug.

Then they told me they wanted to cut Mazzy's hair so that she looked more like a baby.

Ummmm . . . I'm sorry. You don't think my baby looks like a baby?

I let them cut her hair (which wasn't the easiest decision because it was her first haircut) and she did indeed look more like a baby.

Then they took her into another room to get photographed and I sat with the other two moms, staring at one another uncomfortably. We were not allowed to go in.

After the shoot was over, Mazzy emerged happily and we had to wait nine months for our check to arrive in the mail before we knew the outcome. Yes, as long as it took to create her to begin with! If we got a check for just the session fee, she didn't make it. If we got a check for substantially more, Mazzy would soon be staring back at us from the diaper aisle at every grocery store across the country.

I imagined the other moms in my old Mommy & Me class recognizing Mazzy's face when they unloaded diaper packages from their grocery bags. (*I guess she was the cutest baby after all . . .*) I imagined my mother commissioning a fifty-foot model of the diaper package for her front lawn.

But alas, when the envelope finally arrived, it included a check only for the session fee. Mike and I were still hopeful.

"Maybe it's a mistake? And the second check will be sent separately?"

No additional check ever came. There would be no diaper package for us to brag about. No triumphant image to post on Facebook. Our baby's modeling career was over before it even began. Even worse, we never got to see the photos or hear any feedback, so I've always imagined Mazzy's photo wasn't chosen because she wouldn't stop moving during the shoot, making it impossible for the photographer to capture a photo in focus.

God knows that's what has happened to me for the past six years.

My Little Picasso

Mazzy's portraits at age two were really something special. Early on, she started drawing portraits with the finer details of people's faces—circles for eyes and even smaller circles for eyeballs, and then she moved on to noses, nostrils, and even nose hairs.

I don't like to throw the term "child prodigy" around lightly, but I'm perfectly comfortable with "early creative genius."

Here is Mazzy's earliest known piece, created on June 29, 2012. It is titled **"Portrait of Mom."**

Notice the grim face, the bad hair, and the feeling of being perpetually strangled. This is no ordinary work of art by a toddler, but instead a social commentary on motherhood in general.

Her second important piece I've titled **"Papa, Can You Hear Me?"**

The singular nostril and scruff on the chin is typical drawing for a toddler but the detached ear represents something special. I believe this a cry for paternal attention. Perhaps to represent the early mornings when, day after day, only her mother answers her three a.m. wake-up calls. "Don't both parents possess the ability to get out of bed?" she wonders. A thought-provoking question, indeed.

Next we have a work titled **"Self-Portrait."**

Notice how the shaky legs and arms perfectly depict the unsteady stance of a toddler caught between the infantile stage and the progression to full-on child. The large circle between the legs shows the internal struggle of a two-year-old trying to come to terms with the last inevitable toddler milestone—potty training.

And last, we have simply **"Untitled."**

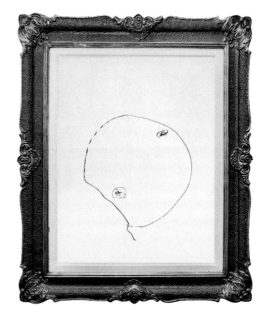

When Mazzy showed me this drawing, I naively believed it to be unfinished and asked who it was going to be.

"Is that Grammy? Poppy? Aunt Ya-Ya, perhaps?"

She looked at me, as if internalizing my critical and cultural limitations for the first time.

"No," she said evenly. "It's a rock with eyes."

It's funny because with second kids, parents tend to keep their expectations in check, instead of glorifying what are really basic skills. At Harlow's preschool parent-teacher conference, the teacher started going on and on about an amazing drawing Harlow did of me. The teacher took ten minutes riffling through papers because she just HAD to show us the drawing, she was so impressed.

"There is such a tremendous level of detail! Representative drawings are actually very rare for a two-year-old."

I don't know what I was expecting her to show me—like an early Leonardo da Vinci sketch. But then she pulled out the picture below and I had to hold myself back from laughing.

I'm not sure we can say "budding Picasso" quite yet.

Every Kid Can't Be President

All parents want to give their kids the most advantages in life. You hear about other parents putting their kids in tons of classes or hiring a tutor to get them into a good preschool and you wonder—am I doing enough?

But all of these classes and tutoring are basically ways parents trick themselves into thinking they can control the future success of their child. You can, in some ways—I've heard having dinner together is a major factor in a child's success. But you can send your kid to Mandarin class at two years old and he could hate every second of it, poisoning him to foreign languages for the rest of his life.

Also, there are countless child psychologists who say "play" is the most important part of a child's early development. So underscheduling your toddler could result in positive effects as well.

In Manhattan, one reason everyone is so on top of their baby's extracurricular activities is because they are all super concerned about getting their kids into the right preschool.

The "right preschool" being the thing that determines the rest of that child's life.

I remember when we applied to preschools for Mazzy. We got forms to fill out that were more in-depth than my college applications.

What adjectives would you use to describe your toddler?

Ummm . . . is "drooly" an adjective?

Please explain your child's personality and temperament.

Hmmmm . . .

She likes to scream bloody murder if her blankie is in the wash and hates eating anything but hot dogs. She wakes up super cranky and demands you put on Bubble Guppies at five a.m., which I do JUST TO MAKE THE WHINING STOP. Her commitment to watching Surprise Egg–opening videos on YouTube is incredibly impressive. But not nearly as impressive as her commitment to her Cars-themed sippy cup. She will cut anyone who offers her milk in anything less.

This was my actual response:

Mazzy is an incredibly bright and creative child who makes a big impression on everyone she meets. She has an active imagination, a great memory, and has been very verbal since an early age. Mazzy adjusts remarkably well to change and new situations. She has always been very social and makes new friends easily. On the playground, she often creates games and gets all her friends involved. She is very inclusive and wants to make sure everyone is having fun.

You know what? Both descriptions are 100 percent true.

And then there's the even more cutthroat world of kindergarten—where you apply to public schools, private schools, gifted-and-talented programs, and Hunter, which is basically a private-school education for FREE, given to only the best and brightest kids in NYC.

Over two thousand kids apply to Hunter and they only take twenty-five girls and twenty-five boys. The pool is first narrowed by a

Hunter-specific test. Anyone who scores over a certain number gets into the second round. I think about 250 kids make the second round, of which Mazzy was one of them. She got two or three points over the required score. When we found out she made it, we were ecstatic.

Then we got the instructions for round two. We were assigned a date and time and told where to bring her. Among all the listed "dos" and "do nots" for the day, the notice said in big bold letters:

DO NOT BRING YOUR CHILD TO YOUR DESIGNATED TIME IF HE/SHE IS SICK. HE/SHE WILL NOT GET IN.

And then underneath:

IF YOU CAN'T MAKE YOUR DESIGNATED TIME, THERE ARE NO MAKEUPS.

The second I read that, I knew what was going to happen. Mazzy was going to get sick on her appointed day.

Which she did.

She was coughing and sneezing and had a nose that was running quicker than you could wipe it.

Did we keep her home?

OF COURSE NOT.

I'm no mathematician, but if the probability is zero Mazzy will get in if she's sick, the probability is less than zero if she doesn't show up at all, right? Seems like you've got nothing to lose at that point.

We took her and I remember wiping her nose around the corner from the school before we went inside so that none of the administrators would see and kick us out. I also made eye contact with another mom across the street inspecting her kid's nostrils and hiding a tissue up his sleeve, so I know Mazzy wasn't

the only sick kid with hopeful parents who forced her to show up for Round #2.

As promised, Mazzy did not get in.

Initially I told myself that if she wasn't sick, she would have had a shot. But then I found out that a friend's kid who did get in had a score WAY, WAY higher than the cutoff score. I felt better after that.

My sister is a school psychologist and told me something that always stuck with me. After Mazzy didn't get into Hunter, I asked her if we made a mistake by dismissing the tutoring thing. Would that have helped Mazzy's chances?

She said, "The worst thing that can happen is that your child ends up at a school where she doesn't really belong."

So basically, if you tutor your kid so that she does well on the test and gets into the school, but she's not quite as gifted and talented as the other kids in attendance, she is going to have a really tough time in kindergarten. This will set her up for failure way more than if you had just let her play at a pace that matched her real abilities.

Not every kid is Hunter material.

Not every kid is going to be president.

Or Picasso.

But you can grow up and go to state school and become a blogger for a living and your mom will still brag about you to her friends.

"Ilana wrote a blog post every day this week! I think we have a future author on our hands!"

And you know what? She's not wrong.

CHAPTER 22

The Secret To Enjoying Parenthood

I always tell my husband it's a good thing we didn't have a boy because he would have expected that boy to be exactly like him. Having girls allows Mike to get to know who they are without putting all his own baggage on them. I think it's an important rule to follow for all parents.

It's not a matter of high or low expectations—it's a matter of no expectations. Discover who your kid is as you go. Your kids will not be who you expect, but the things that amaze us most in life are never the things we expect.

The same goes for your average day. It will be filled with highs and lows, and almost nothing will go according to plan. But that's OK. Kids are unpredictable. Plans are BOOOORING. Life is better with a story to tell and something to laugh about later.

Parenting might be hard, but the upside is that happiness can suddenly be found in the smallest of things. When a car ride goes smoothly or your kid says something especially cute, there is no greater joy. Before you had kids, can you imagine feeling blissful if everyone sat still at a table during dinner? Or if someone brushed their teeth for an appropriate amount of time? Of course not. You'd be insane. But as a parent, the mundane can be pretty magical. That's a gift!

Just the other day, Harlow put on her own shoe and I almost danced on the table. And not in a drunken take-off-my-bra kind of way. Speaking of which—here's a story for you.

When Mazzy was about two, whenever Mike or I came home from work, she would demand we remove our jackets immediately. Something about knowing her working parents weren't walking back out the door, I'm sure.

One day, Mazzy and I were having a little dance party in the living room when Mike walked in the front door. Mazzy (who is always super excited when her dad gets home) screamed, "DANCE, DADDY, DANCE!"

Being the good father that he is, Mike immediately danced over to join us, still wearing his jacket. Mazzy noticed her dad had forgotten the most important step in his "I'm home from work" routine and yelled her usual jacket request.

"Take it off! Take it off!"

So Mike is dancing over to us while simultaneously trying to shimmy out of his jacket and Mazzy is screaming, "Take it off! Take it off!" and all of a sudden I'm like—

"NO NO NO STOP! FOR THE LOVE OF GOD STOP!!!!!!"

Mike suddenly realized what this would sound like to an outsider and we both just started laughing. Like the kind of laughter where your insides hurt and you can barely breathe. Of course, Mazzy didn't understand what was going on (i.e., that she had just treated her dad like a male stripper), but she thought it was hilarious that her parents had a big case of the giggles and joined in, too.

I hadn't laughed that hard since I was a kid myself.

That's another joy of having kids. You get to act like a kid without feeling like an idiot. You can be weird and silly and dance your face off without any drugs at all. I was a really weird kid, and somewhere along the line, I lost that. I stopped making up purposefully terrible songs and using foreign accents for no apparent reason. I grew up and acted like grown-ups are supposed to act in public. But at home, with your kids, you can find your inner weirdo again. It's pretty awesome. And that inner weirdo will teach your kids to be unique and fun and playful and strengthen your relationship with your kids in just as many ways as being the adult in the house.

You also get to experience "firsts" all over again. And not just first steps and first words. I'm talking about the first time your kid sees fireworks or steps in the ocean. The first time you take your kid to Rockefeller Center at Christmas or throw a coin in a fountain to make a wish. All the things that seemed larger than life when you were a kid, but then you grew up and became cynical and jaded and just stopped dreaming.

You get to do everything over again through the eyes of your children. All the wonders of the world appreciated anew.

We don't think twice about a plane flying overhead, but kids think it's amazing, and you know what? They're right! It's a huge hunk of metal with wings and two hundred people traveling inside at a ridiculous speed to a faraway place we've probably never even thought to visit.

Kids make you see that for what it is— unfuckingbelievable.

Don't Appreciate Every Moment

If you are currently a parent, I'm sure at least fifty people have said the following words to you at some point:

"Appreciate every moment because it all goes by so fast."

I hate when people tell me that. I don't want to know that it's going to "pass by in the blink of an eye." That before I know it, I'm going to be eighty and wishing my kids would pick up a phone to call me every now and again. (Or channel me through a holograph or whatever the method is that people get in touch in 2050.)

My kids are three and six and I already think time is flying. But that doesn't make the tantrums and the meltdowns and the general hassle of herding kids any easier.

Hopefully, when my kids are off at Harvard and Oxford studying to be president (or at clown school studying to be a juggler), I'm not going to be home alone thinking about that time Harlow had a meltdown in a crowded Starbucks or the time Mike pinned Mazzy to the floor so I could force-feed her amoxicillin.

Nope, those moments I'm hoping to forget. Or at least remember them with humor and not with the agitation that existed during the actual events.

The secret to enjoying parenthood is not about appreciating every moment. That would be setting your expectations too high, dooming yourself to fail, and doing your kids a huge disservice in the process.

The secret to parenthood is having a selective memory. It's remembering the good stuff.

More important, it's the ability to recognize when you are in a memorable moment and fully appreciating it. Big or small.

Here's a moment I want to remember: When Mazzy was three and Harlow was a few months old, on a particularly beautiful evening, instead of eating dinner and going through our normal bedtime routine, I suggested we all go for a walk outside.

"But I'm in my pajamas!" Mazzy said sensibly.

"Well then, let's take a walk in your pajamas!"

Few things get three-year-olds more excited than the prospect of going out in public in clothes usually reserved for bedtime. Use that. You'll be a hero.

I put Harlow in the carrier, Mike plopped Mazzy on his shoulders, and we strolled around in perfect weather at the most beautiful time of night. Twilight, I believe they call it. Or in photography terms, "the magic hour."

It *was* magical.

When Mazzy asked if we could go to the playground, instead of saying, "Nope, sorry kid, it's too close to bedtime," Mike and I turned to each other, silently agreed, and said, "OK, let's go!"

Mazzy ran around that playground like she owned it, pajamas and all. The sun backlit my husband's silhouette as he hoisted Mazzy in the air and spun her around as she laughed at the darkening sky, all while Harlow slept soundly, nuzzled against my chest.

Sticking to a routine is great and means you have your shit together as a parent, but sometimes breaks in routine are where the wonderful happens.

That was three years ago, and I can still remember how the fading sunlight danced in Mazzy's hair.

Did Mazzy put up a fight when I put her to bed later that night because we had missed her "window"? Did Harlow wake up when I tried to transfer her from the carrier to her crib and then stay up fussing for the next two hours? Did Mike say, "We will pay for this tomorrow," and then "I told you so" the next day when Mazzy threw a fit at breakfast? Probably. But I choose not to remember those moments. I don't like letting a bad ending wipe out all the good stuff that happened leading up to it.

Maybe all happy parents subconsciously pick and choose only the good stuff to remember, which is why twenty years from now we'll also say things like "Cherish every moment" to new parents who will want to kill us.

Something to look forward to, perhaps?

Last summer, Mike and I took the girls kayaking in a small creek on Long Island. I couldn't take my phone, so it's one of the few things I've done with my girls that has no photo documentation.

But I remember it perfectly.

Harlow and Mazzy both wearing sun hats and bright pink life vests and sunglasses. Harlow's little body snug between my legs in the kayak while I paddled. Mazzy and Mike in their own kayak, looking back, yelling for us to keep up. We stopped at a tiny beach and collected shells, skipped rocks, and pointed out horseshoe crabs as the water lapped up on the shore around our feet.

I think it's the happiest I've ever seen my husband.

That's a moment I want us to remember. Hell, I'll let it represent that entire summer if I choose.

I also remember a night when Harlow was about nine months old. We had dinner with my mom and my stepdad, taking a chance by bringing the girls to a restaurant, even though we had sworn we would never attempt eating out again.

I don't know why the restaurant gods smiled down on us that evening, but Mazzy stayed seated and actually ate her meal. Harlow spent the entire time occupied by a drink menu and a spoon. When Mazzy was finished eating, she didn't run around the table pissing off fellow diners, she turned to Harlow and tried to entertain her. To make the evening more amazing, Mazzy's comedy act actually worked. Harlow giggled uncontrollably and I watched my children really play together for the first time.

No one can describe the warm, fuzzy, heart-exploding feeling you get from something as simple as your kids enjoying each other's company. It's just something a parent has to experience for themselves.

There are so many of those moments. Pride and joy and excitement and magic. Like the time I took them both to *Frozen on Ice* and cried through the whole damn thing because I knew how much the experience meant to them. Like a full-on Claire Danes ugly cry.

Those are all once-in-a-lifetime moments. But there are wonderful daily happenings, too.

Harlow doesn't let me leave the house without a hug, kiss, noses, and something she calls "love pats" on my cheeks. Every morning, I ride the bus with Mazzy to school. Talking on the bench at the bus stop is one of my most cherished times of day. At night, Mike throws the girls on the bed for a big tickle fest. On weekends, we have dance parties in the kitchen and eat chocolate chip Minnie Mouse pancakes in the morning. Just cuddling on the couch watching TV on a rainy day is pretty fantastic.

You know what else I love? Carrying my sleeping kids from the car, their weight heavy on my shoulder as I ride the elevator up to our apartment. I love when the door opens and I see us in the mirror. Their little arms hanging over me, their smooshed faces on my shoulder.

Sometimes we get so caught up in the grind—our jobs, routines, errands, discipline, just trying to keep everyone alive and racing to bedtime like it's the finish line at the end of the day—that we forget to notice all the amazing things that happen along the way.

Parenthood is hard. Harder than I ever imagined. But there are incredible moments that I try to recognize and appreciate when they happen, while they are happening.

It is these moments, when I really look at my children, when I share a glance over their heads with my husband, when I take in the fleeting beauty of my entire family, that I hope to remember when I'm old and wondering where all the time has gone.

The Big Secret

We've talked about having no expectations and a selective memory, but are you ready for the biggest secret of all?

Enjoying parenthood is not about trying to be the best mom or having the perfect kids. It's about giving yourself and your kids a break and just letting things play out for what they are sometimes.

It's being OK with being average.

I know, I know, who wants to be average? Sure, strive for something greater—that's up to you. But I'm telling you, having a laid-back approach to parenting is one of the greatest gifts you can give yourself.

Do you know what happens to me when I try to do something extraordinary and it doesn't go my way? I get PISSED.

Accepting my average-ness lets me prepare for the shit show without contributing to it, which means it doesn't escalate to an even worse place.

This doesn't mean you shouldn't try. It just means when you try and it goes no better or worse than a regular day, don't vow never to try again.

Be average. It's okay. This is what will give you the permission to enjoy the good even when it's a struggle. And please understand—it's a struggle for EVERYBODY. I don't care what those "above average" parents tell you.

The attachment parents, the free-range parents, the helicopter parents—we all go through the same shit whether we admit it or not. None of us know more than anybody else. And if we think we do, then our next kid will throw us for a loop. You see, no one can really tell you how to parent because nobody else has YOUR kids. They can talk until they are blue in the face about THEIR kids, but I am willing to bet they aren't an expert on their own kids, either.

Nobody knows what they are doing or has all the answers. We're all just doing the best we can.

Our kids will be our biggest challenges and our greatest joys in life.

Your task is to accept the chaos, laugh through the hard parts, remember the good stuff, and stay strong so that you're still standing in the end when your kids finally go off to college.

Then you get to beg them to come back home to visit you just so you have the pleasure of doing their laundry again.

We can struggle, come up short, and still be awesome moms and dads.

It's all good.

It's parenting.

WHEN YOU'RE THE ONLY ONE PARTICIPATING IN YOUR FAMILY PHOTO

REMARKABLY
AVERAGE PARENT PROBLEMS

WHEN YOU START COUNTING DOWN THE HOURS UNTIL BEDTIME

AND IT'S ONLY NOON.

WHEN YOU MAKE YOUR CHILD PINTEREST-WORTHY LUNCHES

AND THEN THIS IS WHAT YOU PACK FOR YOURSELF.

WHEN IT TAKES THREE HOURS TO WALK ONE BLOCK.

WHEN THE MYLAR BALLOON WON'T DIE

AND YOU HAVE TO KILL IT YOURSELF.

WHEN YOUR DAUGHTER GETS A CUT ON HER MIDDLE FINGER

AND KEEPS SHOWING EVERYBODY.

WHEN YOU'VE GOT TWO SECONDS TO WIPE

BEFORE EVERYONE IN STARBUCKS SEES YOU WITH YOUR PANTS DOWN.

WHEN YOU ASK YOUR TODDLER FOR A PIECE OF HER MUFFIN.

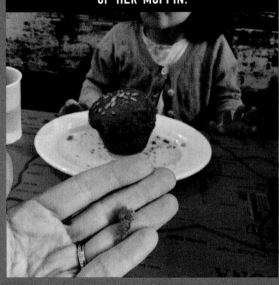

WHEN YOUR KID CAN'T FIND ANY PAPER.

WHEN IT TAKES FOUR GROWN-UPS TO PUT TOGETHER ONE TOY FOR A TWO-YEAR OLD

AND THEY STILL CAN'T DO IT.

WHEN NOBODY WILL STOP LOVING YOU LONG ENOUGH TO ENJOY YOUR MEAL.

WHEN YOU ARE THE ONLY ONE EXCITED ABOUT THE FIRST DAY OF SCHOOL.

WHEN YOUR KID CALLS THE COPS BY ACCIDENT

AND YOU HAVE NO IDEA UNTIL THE COPS SHOW UP AT YOUR DOORSTEP.

WHEN YOU HAVE TO IGNORE YOUR CHILD TO WRITE YOUR BOOK ABOUT PARENTING.

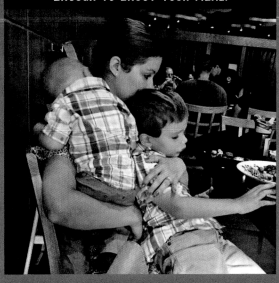

acknowledgments

Mazzy and Harlow, if one day you read this book, please know everything was written with pure love and adoration in my heart. I am so thankful for having two wonderfully smart, funny, unique, loving daughters who give me so many stories I couldn't possibly tell them all.

Mike, for convincing me to take this path—to blog full-time, to build my business, to write this book. Your love and support mean the world to me. Thank you for always finding my keys, refilling my Metrocard and RSVPing to the school picnic on time. And, thank you for reading my blog every day for the past six years. Or at least pretending to.

To my mom and dad (aka Grammy and Poppy) who divorced when I was ten, effectively giving me the gift of a sense of humor as a coping mechanism. BEST GIFT EVER. Mom—thank you for always being there to give me encouragement and guidance. And for setting a shining example of unconditional love that I hope to model for my girls. Dad—thank you for passing on your "underdog" complex and teaching me that working hard is the only way to achieve what you want. Thank you both for bringing Grandsam and Nonna into my life.

To my sister, Myriah, a way above average parent who has saved me from being a total crap parent on more than one occasion. Raising our kids a few blocks away from each other and seeing their relationships grow closer by the day is an absolute dream. DON'T MOVE TO WESTCHESTER!

To Grandma Toby, thank you for forgiving me for the pantaloons post! One of my favorite discoveries from writing my blog was learning my mother-in-law has a wicked sense of humor.

Andrea Barzvi, my literary agent, who encouraged me to write this book. You gave me exactly the push I needed. I'm forever grateful. This book would literally not exist if you hadn't stalked me over Facebook.

To Pam Silverstein for staying up many late nights helping me cut, edit and improve the book until we absolutely weren't allowed to change one more thing. My smartest move was bringing you aboard the team. To Annie Nichtern and Abby Copleston who worked tirelessly to ensure every photo submission was sourced, credited, and officially released for use. And to Cara Braude for your much-needed dance moves.

To the entire team at Abrams for bringing my book to life, including Amy Sly, Claire Bamundo, John Gall, and Kate Lesko. Your knowledge and enthusiasm made me feel the book was in especially good hands. To my editor, Rebecca Kaplan, thank you for always taking the time to assure me that nothing would go out into the world that I wasn't 100 percent proud of.

To Robyn Cohen, thank you for spending your ski vacation proofreading.

Thank you to Ruth Rolon for being the most wonderful caregiver. It is because I'm so comfortable leaving my girls in your confident hands that I was able to pursue my dreams.

Thank you to Seri Kertzner, Karen Alpert, Angie Keiser, Deva Delaporte and HOOBOO for understanding the craziness of the blogging/social media world. Thank you to Emily Shalant, Pam Bernstein, Jessica Corda, and all my friends who don't understand it at all but love me anyway.

Thank you to my readers. Having an audience is the primary reason a newcomer gets a book deal nowadays, so this book couldn't have happened without you. I somehow found a unique online community of sane adults and non-judgmental parents, where the common thread in the comments is always understanding and kindness. If the response I received was different, I probably would have gone back to my cubicle in corporate America long ago. You have made me a better parent, a published author, and with all seriousness—altered the course of my life.